SOCIAL SKILLS FOR TEENS WITH ANXIETY

SOCIAL SKILLS FOR TEENS with ANXIETY

Make Friends and Do Stuff without Feeling Weird

Emily Davenport, MA, ATR-BC, LCAT

callisto publishing
an imprint of Sourcebooks

Illustrations by Mike Mullan
Author photo courtesy of Valerie Terranova Photography
Art Director: Jennifer Hsu & Angela Navarra
Art Producer: Stacey Stambaugh & Hannah Dickerson
Editor: Jeanann Pannasch
Production Editor: Jael Fogle & Rachel Taenzler
Production Manager: David Zapanta & Martin Worthington

Published by Callisto Publishing LLC C/O Sourcebooks LLC
P.O. Box 4410, Naperville, Illinois 60567-4410
(630) 961-3900
callistopublishing.com

Printed and bound in the United States of America.

VP 10 9 8 7 6 5 4 3 2 1

To every teen who experiences
anxiety when they socialize.
May you awaken your resilience
and lovingly embrace your unique spirit.

Contents

Introduction

Welcome. I am *so* happy that you're here. If you feel a bit anxious in social settings, I can relate. When I was a teenager, anxiety sometimes made it hard for me to feel confident in social settings, too. I wish I had known then that it's possible to feel less anxious and more confident. Social skills can be learned and practiced. Many teens just like you experience anxiety around socializing—you are not alone! I want to convey to you that feeling weird doesn't mean that you are weird. There's a difference between a thought and a fact.

This book is based on my experience as a psychotherapist over the past fourteen years. It's also rooted in thirty-nine years of life experience as an imperfect human being. I offer you a unique lens as an art therapist who specializes in using creativity and neuroscience to help teens and adults struggling with anxiety and "big emotions." The framework I use in this book is rooted in creativity, cognitive behavioral strategies, and mind-body practices. I know that's a mouthful. I promise I'll break it down. Throughout this book, you will find unique ways to address anxiety around socializing, including insight-oriented art-making prompts, so have some basic drawing materials handy.

Let's start with a basic question: Why social skills? Well, social skills are pivotal to our connections, and our connections are one of the most powerful indicators of our well-being. You may be feeling pressure to change aspects of your social life and "put yourself out there more." However, managing anxiety in social settings can be difficult. I'm here to tell you that you don't need to fundamentally change who you are to feel less anxious. You also don't need to change all your social behaviors. Throughout this book, we will balance acceptance and change. We will take this journey step-by-step, and I promise to always honor your starting place. I believe wholeheartedly that you've already taken a huge step just by picking up this book. Well done!

From a compassion-focused lens, I will teach you how to skillfully approach anxious thoughts, emotions, body sensations, and action urges. You will learn different ways of responding to anxiety using evidence-based, mindful, and creative tools. You will practice how to embrace your uniqueness (or weirdness) and explore ways to grow. Everyone is capable of growth. I will share down-to-earth examples of how to make that all happen. Let's begin!

HOW TO USE THIS BOOK

You have enough on your plate. That's why I designed this easy-to-use guide to build confidence and connection even with anxiety. You can read it at your own pace, and, if you like, you can also highlight or underline sections that you find interesting. Each of the eight chapters includes tips and reflection questions. There are quizzes and art exercises along the way, too, so it's helpful to gather whatever writing and drawing supplies you may have lying around (pens, colored pencils, crayons, markers, etc.).

First and foremost, my intention is to create a safe space for *you*. There is no wrong way to use this book. If you notice judgments arising about yourself, that's okay. Each time that happens, I want you to label that as a "judgment," not a fact, and move right along. Although this guide may be a helpful resource to manage and decrease anxiety, it does not replace therapy, medication, counseling, or coaching. To get the most out of this book, I encourage you to share your experiences (in and outside this book) with parent(s), caregivers, friends, family, school counselors, therapists, or trusted adults. Likewise, if you're struggling, tell a trusted adult, medical professional, or counselor. Trust me, therapy is not as scary as you may think!

Let me validate a fact. It's hard to learn new things when we're feeling anxious. Humans learn more effectively when they feel safe and relaxed. Therefore, let's try to practice the skills that I will teach you in a relaxed state first. Then, you can "test-drive" these skills when you're feeling heightened increments of anxiety. This is analogous to warming up a car before driving it at 100 miles-per-hour. However, regardless of your anxiety levels, expect to find more than just coping skills and advice in these pages. You'll find hands-on ways to transform anxiety and improve your social skills. Through the mind, body, and creative spirit, I will empower you to develop more helpful narratives and reframe unhelpful ones. I will teach you how to approach yourself with curiosity and compassion. I will remind you of your resilience and strength.

Chapter I

Socializing with Anxiety

You can't change what you are not aware of, so that's where we'll start. Awareness of your anxiety, inner dialogue, and triggers are the first steps toward positive change. In this chapter, we will learn some fundamentals about social skills, anxiety, and different treatment methods. I will be sharing helpful tips and a self-assessment. I will teach you how to recognize signs of anxiety, the various types of anxiety, and different factors that may increase it. After reading this chapter, you will be a little more equipped to address your anxiety. I welcome you to embark on this exciting journey with me and read on.

ENTERING THE DOOR

Darius is a likable fourteen-year-old. He is known as an artist and budding comedian. Even though Darius can sometimes come across as shy, he has many close friends who enjoy his jokes and manga sketches. At the lunch table, Darius is emptying salt packets into his ketchup and daring his friend to eat it. After lunch, Darius whispers to his friends that he really wants to join the art club. When they ask him why he hasn't joined yet, Darius answers, "Eh, it's kinda stupid." Darius knows that's a lie. What his friends don't see is that sometimes Darius's anxiety gets in the way of him trying new things. Darius has gotten as close as walking to the art room door, but then always turns around. Every time he tries to join the art club, his face becomes hot, his chest feels heavy, and he starts to sweat. He feels afraid but doesn't know why.

WHAT DO WE MEAN BY SOCIAL SKILLS?

Social skills are the skills that we use to communicate and connect with others, both verbally and nonverbally. Social skills can be everything from making eye contact to active listening and expressing empathy. We can socialize with our words, and with the tone and pace in which we speak, with gestures, facial expressions, and body language. We can even communicate by the way we dress and style our hair. Some people socialize through sign language, art making, or adaptive technology.

How we socialize is influenced by a combination of factors, including genetics, culture, abilities, environment, experiences, relationships, upbringing, and mass media. There are many skills to help you socialize with anxiety that I'm excited to share with you throughout this book. We will cover everything from identifying anxiety triggers to learning different ways of approaching anxiety. It's my goal to help you understand what drives you and feel more equipped to embrace your uniqueness. Because anxiety doesn't respond well to yelling, or forcing it to go away, I will teach you how to gently ask anxiety to step out of the driver's seat and into the back seat.

I believe that you are the expert on your life. I also believe that you have enough people telling you what you *should* do. A key point in this book is for you to learn how to respond authentically to anxiety given the unique circumstances that arise. You will find plenty of helpful tips and guidance here, but there is no prefabricated formula that you have to follow. That's why I'm inviting you to place emphasis on what works for you.

I want to validate some truths. 1. Socializing comes more naturally to some people than others, and that's okay! 2. People learn social skills at different times and in different ways, and that's okay, too! Let me make this clear: Anxiety around socializing is more common than you think. Even though social skills are vital for connection, it's okay to need a little support.

THE BENEFITS OF LEARNING SOCIAL SKILLS

We are social animals, and we depend on our communities to survive. The ability to form authentic and deep connections is one of the leading predictors of happiness and can even help you live longer. Human beings heal in the context of relationships. Social connections can make us feel seen, heard, and even loved. There are endless benefits to learning effective new ways to socialize, but here's a brief overview.

Learning new tools to use when you're feeling anxious can increase confidence and comfort in social settings. Using the example of Darius, even though he had a close-knit group of friends, joining a new club where he didn't know anyone triggered his anxiety. He didn't feel comfortable introducing himself to new people, and therefore missed out on a meaningful new experience that was important to him. Darius can be coached to use tools to help him reduce anxiety in the moment. He can also learn practical steps to be able to open that art room door and join the art club. Whether it's at school, on the basketball court, or in your future career, social skills are lifelong tools that can help you grow and prosper. Imagine being able to do all the things that you want to do without anxiety holding you back!

INTROVERTS AND EXTROVERTS

How introverted or extroverted you are can influence how and when you socialize. Let's break this down. An extrovert is a person who feels energized when socializing within groups. Socializing invigorates them. Extroverts tend to speak up more often and are generally more outgoing in group settings. They may be eager to try out for the soccer team, for example, even if they don't know any of the players.

On the other hand, an introvert is a person who feels more depleted when they socialize within large groups or in situations where they don't know people. This doesn't mean that introverts don't enjoy socializing, it simply happens to tire them out a bit more. Introverts tend to enjoy one-on-one conversations more, and they may be a bit cautious about joining that same soccer team. To be clear, being more introverted does not mean that you have social anxiety. If you're more introverted, it simply means that you benefit from taking time to recharge.

Many people fall in varied spots along the introvert/extrovert spectrum. Oftentimes, people are not 100 percent extrovert or 100 percent introvert. Whether you're more introverted or extroverted, both have pros and cons. The world needs both, and one is not better than the other.

READINESS RATING

Rate how ready you are to embrace the following changes. Place the corresponding letter next to each statement:

R = Ready; U = Unsure; N = Not yet

1. I am willing to notice when I'm worrying, and label it as a "worry thought." ☐
2. I am willing to notice when my body feels tense and stretch when that happens. ☐
3. I am willing to notice self-judgments, and label them as "judgments, not truths." ☐
4. When I have an urge to give up, I am willing to take a deep breath and keep going. ☐
5. I am willing to engage in the practices in this book. ☐
6. I am willing to learn how to socialize with more ease and confidence. ☐
7. I am willing to learn about anxiety and how it affects socializing. ☐

Now it's your turn. Create a self-statement that you are willing to explore.

I am willing to: ______________________________

TAKE A DEEP BREATH

Sometimes just reading about anxiety can increase anxiety. If that happens, it's okay. I invite you to keep reading. By doing that, you're already practicing a skill called approaching your anxiety that can help manage anxiety. We'll talk more about approaching your anxiety later, but first, let's dive more into anxiety.

Anxiety is an emotion characterized by intense, persistent worry and fear about a perceived or actual threat. It lives not only in our emotional world but also in our bodies' sensations, thoughts, urges, and actions. Anxiety can affect how we feel and think about ourselves and how we socialize. Anxiety can make you speak quickly and blurt things out, or freeze and stay silent. It can look like not knowing what to do with your hands, laughing uncontrollably, or feeling like you always have to urinate. As a fellow human being, I can validate that it's normal to want to avoid painful experiences. However, there's pain that produces growth, and pain that just produces more pain.

Avoiding anxiety ends up *strengthening* anxiety. Avoidance creates long-term pain. An annoying fact, I know. However, anxiety is not our enemy, and it serves an important purpose. In other words, you can learn how to live with your anxiety and not let it take over your life. I will teach you how to surf the anxiety waves and resist the urge to give into anxious action urges. I will also teach you how to use life preservers (skills) if you fall in the murky anxiety waters.

WHAT CAUSES ANXIETY?

You probably want to get rid of anxiety. I hear you. However, we all need anxiety. Hear me out. Anxiety is designed to help you. Anxiety can propel you to study harder, memorize important information, and protect you from danger. It is your internal alarm system and comes from a part of your brain called the amygdala. Your ancestors relied on anxiety and fear to respond to danger through a fight, flight, or freeze response. If your ancestors saw a saber-toothed tiger lurking behind them, they would throw rocks (fight), run (flight), or play dead (freeze).

Most of us do not live in imminent danger of being eaten. However, stressful experiences can create the same action urges that our ancestors once experienced. Sometimes, we can interpret everyday situations and social interactions as threatening, even when we're not in danger. This can activate our fight, flight, or freeze response. There are many factors that influence how easily triggered our anxiety alarm system is. Our genetics, upbringing, environment, habits, and even nutrition can influence anxiety. Teens may be more vulnerable to experiencing anxiety because their brains and bodies are changing, social circles are widening, and responsibilities are increasing.

Think of anxiety as a superhero who tries to rescue you, even when you don't need rescuing. Your anxiety superhero may say, "This doesn't seem safe. Let's go home." This superhero may be very practiced at protecting you. That's okay—after all, it's just doing its job. However, if you feel like your anxiety superhero never leaves you alone, or is working overtime, then it's time to re-evaluate the relationship. I will teach you how to decrease anxiety's power and decline its commentary. You can learn to say, "Thanks, but no thanks, anxiety." At the end of the day, your power lies in how you respond to your anxiety.

SWEATING, SHAKING, BLUSHING

Anxiety activates the body's autonomic nervous system (ANS), which regulates bodily functions, including breathing, digestion, and heart rate. Physical signs of anxiety can be stomach pain, rapid breathing, increased heart rate, and sweating.

These body sensations may feel uncomfortable, but they are designed to protect us from danger. If your heart starts racing, that's your body increasing blood flow, which prepares you to run (flee). It's common to become anxious about the possibility of becoming anxious. For example, you might experience anxiety while thinking about an upcoming presentation—not because you don't feel confident, but purely out of fear that the class might see your anxiety symptoms. Although these sensations may feel overwhelming, there are ways to manage them. Body sensations do not have to dictate your actions. Therefore, how you respond to these sensations influences their power. Let me end with a powerful note about something called neuroplasticity.

Neuroplasticity is a term used to describe your brain's ability to change and create new pathways in response to your experiences. Therefore, if you've been avoiding situations that trigger anxiety, those "avoidance" pathways have been reinforced simply because they are practiced a lot. You can also regularly practice gently approaching anxiety triggers, which creates new pathways and results in less anxiety in the long term. This is analogous to working out. When you work out a new muscle group, it becomes sore. Likewise, your mind is just another muscle. Parts of your brain are simply in better shape than others. Just because a muscle feels sore doesn't mean you should stop doing that exercise. In the same way, approaching anxiety can feel uncomfortable, but that doesn't mean you should stop. Mild to moderate discomfort might be a sign that you're doing something right. Just remember that the more you practice socializing skillfully with a plan, the easier socializing will become.

If you experience intense anxiety or panic in response to any of these practices, or if you notice that it feels impossible to achieve your social goals due to debilitating anxiety or fear, I recommend taking a pause and asking your parent or parents to connect you with a mental health therapist. You can also visit your school counseling center for support. To be clear, some amount of discomfort can produce growth, however exposing yourself to situations and practices that cause panic, intense fear, or fight, flight, or freeze responses can be harmful and is counterproductive. This simply means that you may benefit from professional support to help you reach your goals and socialize with more ease and confidence.

The Cold Cure

Before we start, let's remember to practice new skills when you're feeling somewhat relaxed and centered. Once you're comfortable with a new skill, test-drive it with different increments of anxiety. The following is an exciting evidence-based coping skill that stops intense anxiety and panic in its tracks. This exercise is traditionally done by submerging your face in cold water. It's a distress tolerance skill that should be used in situations where anxiety feels intolerable, or so overwhelming that you feel you cannot cope. It's an effective tool to first practice at home.

Go to the kitchen or bathroom and put some very cold water in a zip-top bag or on a washcloth. You can also use a bag of frozen vegetables. If you're at school, you can use a sink or water fountain. If you're feeling intense anxiety, you can try this practice sitting on the ground up against a wall or lying down. Now, breathe in, close your eyes, and place the cold water on your eyes and cheeks. Hold your breath for about ten to fifteen seconds, then breathe out. If it starts hurting, or you can't hold your breath, then adjust accordingly and don't push yourself. It shouldn't hurt.

The benefits of this exercise include slowing down your heart rate and significantly decreasing physical symptoms of anxiety. This works by activating something called your vagus nerve, which switches on "rest and digest" signals that are the opposite of fight, flight, and freeze. Repeat as needed. If you have heart problems, please consult your doctor before trying this exercise.

WHEN ANXIETY FEELS OUT OF CONTROL

Anxiety can range from frequent worry thoughts to debilitating panic. Different situations trigger different anxiety responses. Some teens have ongoing anxiety that negatively affects how they relate to themselves and others, and their ability to make friends. In such cases, they may have social anxiety disorder, generalized anxiety disorder, another type of anxiety disorder, or none! There is a huge range of stress responses that depend on several circumstances; thus, it's important to get clarity from a professional if you're struggling; I cannot diagnose you.

Wherever you land on the anxiety spectrum, I bet you've been trying hard to cope. Please know that you may just have a sensitive anxiety alarm system. Your anxiety may be doing a really good job "protecting" you. This does not mean that there's anything wrong with you. It just means that you might need a little support and some new skills. Let's also acknowledge that it is very difficult to address anxiety if your basic needs are going unmet or if you're exposed to unsafe situations or unsafe people. I've worked with teens who do not have consistent food or a safe place to live. I've also supported teens who are being emotionally, physically, or sexually abused. If this is true for you, ask for help from a school counselor or a trusted adult. Asking for emotional support is no different than asking for help if you have an ear infection. Our brain is just another part of our bodies. Whatever your lived experience is, remember that humans are resilient, and change is possible.

GENERALIZED ANXIETY DISORDER

Think of generalized anxiety disorder (GAD) as a slow-cooker type of anxiety; it's always on, simmering slowly in the background of your life. It can cool down or heat up, but it always seems to be there. GAD is excessive and ongoing anxiety or worry about everyday life, future events, and what may seem like small matters. If you have GAD, these worries tend to interfere with most aspects of your life. For example, people with GAD might worry about friendships, school performance, the safety of family members, their future career, or what they're going to wear next week. To mitigate these anxieties, they may strive to be "perfect" to avoid making mistakes.

Teens with GAD may be fidgety, restless, tired, and tense. They may have trouble relaxing or sleeping. They may also experience headaches and stomachaches. GAD can occur with other mental health symptoms, such as depression or post-traumatic stress disorder (PTSD). There is a difference between someone who feels anxious and someone who struggles with GAD. It's healthy to feel anxious sometimes. We need anxiety to protect us. However, if you notice that you're feeling intense worry or anxiety symptoms more days than not, and it's affecting your life, then it's time to ask for help.

SOCIAL ANXIETY DISORDER

If GAD is like a slow-cooker type of anxiety, then social anxiety disorder (SAD) is a gopher type of anxiety. Gophers pop out of their little grassy homes then pop back in. SAD is an anxiety that is more pronounced in social situations. That's not to say that people with SAD have disappearing anxiety. SAD is more than feeling shy. It's a long-standing and intense fear of social situations that impacts your life. It can present as fear of being judged, worrying if people like you, or feeling anxious when you're around people. If you have SAD, you may dread raising your hand in class, speaking in public, introducing yourself, or looking someone in the eye. It's typical to have days where you feel shy or awkward or don't want to speak up. That doesn't necessarily mean that you have SAD.

In social situations, teens with SAD tend to experience physical symptoms of anxiety, such as shortness of breath, increased heart rate, dizziness, jitteriness, tension, nervousness, or nausea. They may rehearse what they're going to say before they speak. They may feel self-conscious most of the time and may have been struggling with these symptoms for many months or years. If you notice intense, ongoing, and overwhelming anxiety or fear about socializing, then it's worth exploring SAD further.

FINDING YOUR STARTING POINT

Let's gauge your personal starting point. This is not a formal assessment or a diagnostic tool. This quiz is meant to be a self check-in to empower you by helping you understand your experiences. Write the number that corresponds with your response at the end of each line, then tally your total score:

0 = Not true; 1 = Somewhat true; 2 = Absolutely true

1. I tend to worry about the future every day. ______
2. I have trouble relaxing and/or sleeping most nights. ______
3. I worry about what others think of me most of the time. ______
4. I tend to avoid situations or activities because they make me feel anxious. ______
5. I often feel jittery, uneasy, tense, nauseous, or breathless. ______
6. Before I go to bed, my mind feels like it's racing. ______
7. I tend to feel panicky, tense, and/or "on edge." ______
8. It's hard for me to socialize. ______

If you scored 7 or more, then it's an indicator that you may benefit from speaking to someone you trust about your experiences.

STRATEGIES FOR MOVING FORWARD

Luckily, anxiety is treatable. While this book is not a replacement for therapy and is not treatment, I will share easy-to-use strategies and tools to help you manage anxiety and socialize with more ease. These techniques are designed for teens dealing with anxiety. We'll be diving into cognitive behavioral therapy (CBT) strategies, dialectical behavior therapy (DBT) skills, mindful and somatic techniques, and art therapy. A mouthful, I know!

Here's a quick synopsis of these modalities. Cognitive behavioral therapy (CBT) is a structured treatment approach that places emphasis on how our thoughts and perceptions influence our behaviors and emotions. Dialectical behavior therapy (DBT) is a form of CBT that emphasizes skill-building rooted in the categories of interpersonal effectiveness, distress tolerance, mindfulness, and emotion regulation. The various mindfulness-based and somatic techniques that I will mention combine frameworks of Buddhist and somatic psychology (psychology that focuses on the physical body) along with mindful self-compassion. I'll also refer to elements of art therapy. Art therapy is a form of psychotherapy that uses creative self-expression through various art media. Although we won't be engaging in psychotherapy, I'll share with you valuable take-homes derived from these helpful methods.

THE ABCS OF CBT AND DBT

Let's break down CBT and DBT a little further. CBT is based on the belief that our thoughts and our interpretations of those thoughts affect how we feel and act. In CBT, you focus on changing the way you think and perceive situations. CBT assesses how realistic, or distorted, certain thoughts are and encourages you to develop alternative thoughts that are more realistic and/or helpful. CBT believes that if you learn to change the way you think and perceive experiences, you may feel less anxious (because you are less likely to behave in ways that increase anxiety.)

Since DBT is a form of CBT, there are some similarities between the two. However, unlike CBT, DBT focuses on accepting opposites (also known as dialects). This may sound like, "I love my mom and

I'm angry with my mom" or "I'm scared of socializing AND I can socialize with confidence." Therefore, it's not always so much about change, but more about balancing acceptance and change. In DBT, you learn skills to help you increase mindfulness of your body sensations, emotions, urges, thoughts, and behaviors to help you regulate, accept, and/or change them. You may examine or challenge your thoughts, but you will also learn skills to increase your social effectiveness and tolerate distress.

BREAKING DOWN ART THERAPY AND MINDFUL AND SOMATIC THERAPY

Sometimes, we need alternatives to "talking it out." This is where creative, mindful, and somatic therapies come in. Let's start with art therapy. Art therapy is a form of psychotherapy that uses the art-making process for self-expression to foster well-being. Art therapy is an effective modality for children, teens, and adults. When we make art in the context of a therapeutic relationship, we're connecting our minds and bodies, conscious and unconscious. Therefore, in this way, art therapy offers unique avenues to healing that most cognitive therapies cannot. Art therapists hold master's degrees in art therapy and are clinically trained to use the art and verbal therapies to address issues such as anxiety.

Mindful and somatic interventions emphasize nonjudgmental awareness and attention to the present moment using the mind-body connection. These techniques create space to notice and experience emotions and body sensations and shift your focus toward curiosity and acceptance and away from judgment and change. When something cannot be changed and you continue to fight for change, it amplifies pain. These frameworks help you decrease emotional pain by learning to resist the urge to fight reality. Emphasis is placed on noticing thoughts, emotions, and body sensations and avoiding judgements. These methods also use the body and breath as tools to help you self-soothe. They are anchored in the belief that our bodies hold stories and lean towards compassion-focused inquiry of our mind-body experiences instead of change-based interventions.

Reflection Questions

1. List one thing that you have learned about anxiety.

____

____

____

2. List one belief that you hold about yourself that might not be true. Next to that belief, rate your "believability" rating, on a scale of 0 to 100. 100 = I believe that it's 100 percent true; 0 = I believe that it's 0 percent true.

____

____

____

3. Label one thing that might be affecting your ability to socialize the way that you want to or feel confident socializing.

____

____

____

Chapter 2

Your Personal Starting Point

I get *really* excited talking about triggers, behaviors, goals, and values! Why? Because I know firsthand that unraveling these topics can help you increase confidence in social settings. In this chapter, we will identify what triggers your anxiety and take a deep dive into your responses, goals, and values. I'll show you how these topics are important pieces of your anxiety puzzle. After all, to complete a puzzle you need all of the pieces, so let's not leave any out. In this chapter, we'll take a broad look at all the pieces that affect anxiety around socializing. But first, just remember that the goal is not to get rid of your anxiety altogether. The goal is to not allow anxiety to dictate your actions, or prevent you from doing the things that you want to do or being the person who you want to be. We are here to welcome anxiety as a gentle whisper in the background, not a screaming fire engine (unless we really need that alarm because there's a legitimate fire).

SAM LOVES DOGS

Sam (they/them) has been dreaming about becoming a dog trainer for many years. Stacks of colorful dog training books line their bedroom walls. They have a natural ability to make even the most nervous dogs feel comfortable. Sam recently applied for a volunteer position at the local animal shelter. They have an upcoming interview but want to cancel it. Why? Because Sam's anxiety is triggered when they have to talk to new people. The morning of the interview, Sam's anxiety surges. They can't stop checking their phone as their heart pounds. Sam has a strong urge to stay home but decides to pull through.

They show up for the interview wearing their favorite pair of jeans. Even though Sam has trouble making eye contact, they're able to clearly and passionately express why they're a good candidate for the position. A few days later, Sam receives notice that they got the position. Sam's eyes well with tears of happiness. They did it!

TRIGGERS

Does your anxiety seem to pop up out of nowhere? I remember what that was like. It can leave you feeling helpless. However, there are almost always triggers to anxiety. Let's figure out what anxiety triggers are and explore a little theory behind what makes these triggers predictable. People experience different levels of anxiety at different times. What triggers one person's anxiety may look completely different for another. It's important to learn what may or may not trigger you.

Anxiety triggers can be emotions, thoughts, body sensations, urges, experiences, or even our five senses. Anxiety triggers can be people, places, memories, or even food. Our perceptions, such as perceiving failure or disappointment, can also trigger anxiety. It can feel like a mild flutter in your tummy, or like an intense pounding in your chest. Everyday choices can affect how quickly or intensely we experience anxiety. Our food affects our mood, and certain vitamin deficiencies can increase anxiety. Even dehydration can increase susceptibility to anxiety! It may seem like a lot is working against us, but here's how we can take the power back. It starts with mindfulness.

Mindfulness essentially means nonjudgmental awareness and attention to the present moment. The opposite of mindfulness is something called autopilot: doing things automatically, with little awareness of what you're doing. When you're on autopilot, anxiety can seem to pop up out of nowhere. Therefore, autopilot makes anxiety unpredictable. When you are mindful, anxiety is much more predictable; you have the power to cope ahead and practice different ways of responding. Exploring triggers from a mindful lens is a step toward putting yourself in the driver's seat, not your anxiety! The goal isn't to get rid of triggers; it's to mindfully acknowledge and label your triggers so you can respond more effectively to them. Start by identifying and labeling your anxiety triggers.

One tip to keep in mind though: Notice the urge to examine every sign of anxiety. The aim here is to practice a gentle noticing, not to "hook into" and magnify every possible anxiety flutter. There's a difference between observing and getting caught up in examining our thoughts and emotions. It may help to anchor yourself in a slow, deep belly breath every time you notice an anxiety thought or sensation. Observe it floating past like a cloud and then move on. If the anxiety thought or sensation starts to build and you find yourself overwhelmed, you can try the cold cure skill or another grounding skill that I will talk about shortly! So stay tuned.

WHERE DOES ANXIETY LIVE IN YOUR BODY?

Part 1: Where do you feel anxiety in your body? Do you feel anxiety in your heart, head, chest, and/or hands? Pay attention to where you notice sensations. In the body outline, choose a color that represents anxiety and color in where you feel anxiety in your body. There are no right or wrong answers. Feel free to use markers, colored pencils, or anything else you have on hand.

Part 2: Connect to a place in your body that feels safe, relaxed, or at ease. It could be a toe, hand, or any other area. Focus on that sensation for a moment. Now choose a color that represents safety, relaxation, and ease and depict where this lives in your body and what shape it looks like. Color in and around any areas that need a sense of safety and relaxation.

Part 3: Write a list of what triggers your anxiety and what also makes you feel safe and at ease.

continued ›

Triggers:

____

____

____

____

____

____

Here are examples of triggers:

- Perceiving that someone is mad at you
- Feeling tired, hungry, or dehydrated
- Crowds
- Meeting new people
- Joining a new activity
- Being called on in class
- Starting a conversation
- Upcoming events such as graduation, a school dance, or a big test
- Witnessing family members argue

Things that make me feel relaxed and at ease:

____

____

____

____

____

____

Here are examples:

Petting my dog

Watching my favorite show

Getting a hug

Reading a book

Talking to a friend

COMMON TRIGGER RESPONSES

In response to our anxiety triggers, we often rely on strategies that help alleviate our anxiety. This makes sense. If a pan is hot, we learn not to touch it. However, if we get burned once, and then refuse to ever touch a pan again, or use layers of oven mitts in order to avoid getting burned again, then cooking becomes nearly impossible. It makes sense to avoid burns. As our burn heals, we can try to cook again. In the same way, you can learn how to engage in social situations instead of avoiding them or using protective layers that make socializing more cumbersome.

"I CAN'T GO TODAY . . ." AND OTHER AVOIDANCE BEHAVIORS

Avoidance behaviors are intuitive ways to cope with pain. Avoidance behaviors are common actions that temporarily reduce anxiety by keeping us away from situations that increase it. However, the very act of avoidance prevents us from experiencing a full range of opportunities and experiences. The goal is not to get rid of all your avoidance behaviors—it's to understand which ones are the most problematic and focus on changing those.

I'll call myself out and say that I used to engage in a lot of avoidance behaviors, and sometimes I still do. For the most part, I've learned to recognize which ones are problematic. Avoidance behaviors can include oversleeping, showing up late, avoiding eye contact, skipping activities, choosing the seat farthest from the teacher, putting your head down in class, bullying, ignoring requests, staying quiet, acting like you don't know how to do something, refusing to try new things, or making excuses.

Avoidance behaviors do temporarily work. You probably experience immediate relief by avoiding your anxiety triggers. But do you want to feel less anxious on a day-to-day basis? Do you want to go to new places or meet new people without feeling panicky? If so, then it's time to explore which avoidance behaviors need to be reevaluated. We learn by doing. When any behavior is practiced over and over, it becomes a habit. If you keep avoiding your anxiety triggers, you're reinforcing anxiety and making your anxiety worse.

Anxiety's job is to alarm you with its "danger radar." However, sometimes its radar is inaccurate or on overdrive. When you practice following your anxiety's advice over and over, it strengthens avoidance and therefore anxiety, too. This is also where anxiety about anxiety can pop up. Therefore, you can feel anxious about the possibility of feeling anxious. This results in spending excessive time and energy figuring out how to keep avoiding. This is a common and depleting cycle. No wonder you're tired!

CHECKING YOUR PHONE . . . AND OTHER SAFETY BEHAVIORS

We all want to feel safe. Safety behaviors are coping behaviors that temporarily increase a sense of safety or security. They are used to reduce fear or anxiety. Teens often rely on safety behaviors when faced with anxiety because it makes them feel comforted. The theory behind safety behaviors makes total sense—your body is trying to help you self-soothe.

Just as I'm not asking you to get rid of all your avoidance behaviors, I'm also not asking you to banish all of your safety behaviors. Again, I encourage you to explore which ones are the most problematic or disruptive, and address those first. Why do we need to address safety behaviors? Because safety behaviors tend to amplify fear and anxiety. These behaviors can look like wearing earbuds or sunglasses, constantly checking your phone, carrying a water bottle everywhere, keeping your coat on, picking your nails, playing with your hair, relying on your favorite sweater for comfort, over-preparing to avoid criticism, constantly apologizing, or consuming alcohol.

Many of your safety behaviors aren't helping you. When you engage in safety behaviors, you're reinforcing (or practicing) the idea that certain experiences or people are not safe. Safety behaviors are helpful and protective if they help you avoid things like going into a dark alley by yourself or accepting a ride from a stranger. However, as you have probably learned by now, some of these protections are amplified and keep us from living our lives to the fullest.

Safety behaviors can directly interfere with social skills because they can push people away. Would you want to try and start a conversation with someone in class who has earbuds in and sunglasses on? Probably not. It would be very hard to start a conversation with that person. I might ask this person to give up one of their safety behaviors to start off. Or, I might ask that person to share an earbud with a classmate so that they can socialize and use that safety behavior in a different way.

Anchor into the Present Moment

Anxiety takes you out of the present moment. This mindful coping skill will bring you back in. Practicing this skill will leave you feeling calmer and more centered. You can practice it anywhere with no equipment needed. All you'll need is yourself. The goal is to help you regulate your anxiety, allowing you to gently approach your triggers rather than avoid them. Let's start!

Slowly turn your head from side to side as you look around the room (or wherever you are). Name three things that you can see, three things that you can hear, and three things that you can physically touch (and touch those things). An example of this might sound like: "doorknob, light, mirror, train, wind, people talking, chair, pillow, and blanket."

If you want to get fancy, you can add in one thing that you smell and one thing that you can taste. Fun fact: Super sour candy can reduce anxiety by increasing salivation! So, throw in some sour candy!

OUR VALUES DRIVE US

Let's talk about what you value. Values are an individual's beliefs that guide and motivate their attitudes and actions. Values influence our behaviors, worldview, and priorities. Identifying values can also help us face our social fears. Personally, I have trouble motivating myself to do something if I don't understand the value in doing it. Finding your own personalized "why" is essential to move toward more confident social connections.

Here are some examples of values: *adventure, environmentalism, equal rights, animal rights, honesty, belonging, creativity, culture, courage, community, connection, compassion, patience, friendships, family, heritage, health, humor, open-mindedness, safety, respect, education, justice, growth, sports, loyalty, religion, kindness, self-expression* (and more)!

Identify one thing that you value. Now, how does this value relate to socializing? It may not seem obvious, so ask yourself, "Does my anxiety around socializing ever get in the way of living aligned with my values?" It's common to act in a way that's misaligned with our values. We are left feeling unfulfilled, disconnected, unhappy, and experiencing a sense of unease. Those feelings are your intuition pushing you to align your actions with your values.

Let's revisit our friend Sam, who values animals, and Darius, who values art. Sam's anxiety made it hard for them to volunteer at the animal shelter (but they pushed through—yay), and Darius's anxiety made it hard for him to join the art club. Likewise, if you value friendship but don't want to call a friend back because talking on the phone is an anxiety trigger, that's another example of our values not aligning with our actions. I know some values may seem unrelated to socializing, but I encourage you to be a detective and find the missing links!

IDENTIFYING YOUR VALUES

Part 1: Read each prompt and jot down as many answers as possible. Write quickly, and don't overthink it. There are no wrong answers. At the end of each category, look back and label a "value theme": (*See examples of value themes on page 27.*)

Make a list of all the people, places, or things that make you smile:

____

____

____

____

____

____

What do all of these have in common? That's your value theme! ______________________________

____

____

____

____

____

Make a list of all the things that are important to you:

What do all of these have in common? That's your value theme!

continued ›

Make a list of all the things that you're good at:

____

____

____

____

____

____

____

____

What do all of these have in common? That's your value theme! ____

____

____

____

____

____

Part 2: Create a value shield. Based on your part 1 answers, draw symbols or depictions of your value themes inside your value shield. Your values can act as a protection or a guide to drive your actions. If you value music, art making, and animals, you might draw a microphone, paintbrush, and cat. Use any colors or materials that you'd like!

MAKING SOCIAL GOALS

Let's brainstorm goals for your social life. When picking goals, make sure that they are actionable and specific. Let's set a long-term goal of making a best friend. Now, let's break this goal down into achievable short-term goals. Although there are a lot of different types of goals, short-term goals are goals that you can accomplish within days or weeks. Long-term goals are goals that you can accomplish in weeks or months or even years. Sometimes long-term goals can even take years to accomplish, and that's okay. Short-term goals help you achieve your long-term goals.

Let's say that you have a long-term goal of making a best friend. To achieve that, we can work on a number of short-term goals. The first step might be to identify who you want to be best friends with. The next step might be to make eye contact and smile at them three times a week. After that, if they're receptive and smile back, the next step might be to start up small talk. After small talk, you may feel brave enough to invite them to hang out outside school! As you can see, almost anything can be broken down into small, achievable steps. Remember to start simple; a "hello" can go a long way. When choosing a friend, try engaging with peers who share similar interests. Make it a goal to get to know them better by asking a question or commenting on something that you observe about them.

When looking for friends, choose to engage with people who you have something in common with. Maybe they share an interest with you. This makes putting yourself out there easier! If these examples sound too intimidating, another short-term goal might be to practice imagining yourself successfully speaking to a potential friend. Play it out like a movie in your head. Imagine it going well!

Reflection Questions

Now let's set some actionable, specific, and achievable goals:

1. What is one long-term goal that you can set for yourself?

2. What are two short-term goals that you can set for yourself (to meet the long-term goal)?

3. What, if anything, do you perceive is holding you back from achieving this goal, and are there any steps that you can take to remove roadblocks?

Chapter 3

Brain Training: Challenge Your Thoughts

Sometimes we treat thoughts as truths. However, just because you think it, doesn't mean it's true! There are patterns of thinking that can be unhelpful and problematic. I call these "thought traps," because they can trap you in anxiety cycles. Thought traps are thought patterns based on assumptions instead of evidence. They tend to be exaggerated, distorted, irrational, or overly biased. Certain thoughts become unhelpful when we interpret them as truths and let them dictate our actions. In this chapter, we'll label and challenge unhelpful thinking patterns. We'll also discuss approaching your anxiety and learn how to respond to thought traps effectively.

JESSE PUSHES FORWARD

Jesse scans the basketball court before bending down to re-lace her sneakers. She notices three girls playing basketball. Jesse timidly approaches them, but they appear to ignore her. She feels absolutely devastated. In reality, the girls are so focused on their game that they don't really notice Jesse. The following are two potential responses and interpretations of this event. Which one is most helpful?

Option A: Jesse decides to play by herself. As she's practicing her layups, all she can think about is how much the girls must hate her. She wonders if it's worth playing basketball at all.

Option B: Jesse takes a deep breath and places her shoulders back and her chin up. She approaches the girls directly. Her anxiety rises as she says, "Hey, can I play with you?" "Sure," one of the girls responds. As the girl throws Jesse the ball, she exhales, and her anxiety softens.

UNHELPFUL THINKING PATTERNS

Anxiety increases when we believe in and/or act on exaggerated, irrational, and overly biased thoughts. In option A, Jesse chose to believe that the girls hated her, although she didn't have much evidence for this assumption. This interpretation made her feel bad about herself. Jesse's thought trap, or unhelpful thinking pattern, made socializing harder for her. It made Jesse feel unnecessarily self-conscious and anxious in that social situation. Option A led Jesse to rely on avoidance and safety behaviors. Option B led Jesse to avoid the thought trap that the girls did not like her because she had no evidence for it. As a result, she pushed past her anxiety and had a positive social interaction.

Common thought traps tied to anxiety in social settings are *catastrophizing*, *mind reading*, *spotlighting*, and *all-or-nothing-thinking*. We'll discuss how to identify and challenge unhelpful thought patterns so you can move through social situations with less anxiety. How do we know which thoughts to pay attention to? Thoughts ebb and flow like the tides of the ocean. They can be biased, unbiased, and everything in between. Thoughts can be your own or influenced by another person's voice. Thoughts can be meaningful or meaningless. Keep in mind that all your thoughts are welcome here. None of your thoughts are "bad." So, as we consider unhelpful thinking patterns, we'll discuss which thoughts are important to notice. The goal is to train ourselves to recognize patterns of thinking that interfere with socializing with more ease and confidence.

CATASTROPHIZING

Catastrophizing is when we automatically go to the absolute worst-case scenario. This is accompanied by thoughts of the most devastating outcomes. An example of catastrophizing might be: *"If I fail this test, then I won't graduate, and I'll be a total failure in life."* Catastrophic thinking can also sound like: *"Because I didn't get invited to the school dance, no one likes me. No one ever will."* Catastrophizing can cause anxiety, and anxiety can cause catastrophizing. It's a self-perpetuating cycle. Every human tends to catastrophize from time to time. It's yet another protective mechanism. However, like all protective mechanisms, it can go on overdrive and develop superpowers if we don't practice balancing it out with facts. Catastrophizing can be reinforced if we practice listening to and acting on our catastrophic thoughts. Catastrophizing is certainly one of the most common thought traps that keeps teens from socializing. However, remember, just because you think it, doesn't mean it's true! To address catastrophizing, look for facts.

MIND READING

Mind reading is when you assume that you know what others are thinking. Mind reading is a common thought trap that people with anxiety around socializing experience. Mind reading is an adaptive skill that allows us to try to anticipate the actions of others to stay safe. If a cave person sees a look of surprise from someone in their group, that alerts them to pause and scan for danger. That cave person may interpret the look of surprise as a danger cue and feel unsafe. Therefore, interpreting what others think has a biological origin. But what if we conclude that others don't like us, or are judging us because of a slight change in facial expression? If you're practiced at mind reading, you might automatically assume that people are angry with you or dislike you, even when that's not true. To combat mind reading, ask questions and challenge your assumptions.

SPOTLIGHTING

Ever get the feeling that everyone is looking at you? Spotlighting is a term used to define the tendency to overestimate how much people notice your actions, appearance, or mistakes. Let's say that a few hairs are sticking out of your ponytail. If you're spotlighting, you may think, *everyone must have noticed my hair*. However, in reality, very few people, if any, probably noticed (or cared). Let's say that you're speaking in class and mispronounce a word. A spotlighting response might be to think that everyone is laughing at you behind your back. In reality, some people may notice, but they probably won't think much of it. Your perception is different from how others perceive you. Most people are not going to go home and say, "Guess what, Marly mispronounced a word today." Remember that your perception is different from others. Just because you notice mistakes doesn't mean that others will.

ALL-OR-NOTHING THINKING

All-or-nothing thinking relies on extremes and is sometimes described as black-and-white thinking. It's a type of thought trap where a person interprets situations to an exaggerated degree. These snap judgments can sound like, "They either love me, or hate me." Or, "I had the absolute worst day or the absolute best day" (no in-between). The more we rely on all-or-nothing thinking, the harder socializing can be. If we don't leave any wiggle room for *maybes* or *in-betweens*, we miss out on a lot of opportunities to socialize. There are a lot of gray areas in life. We can be a tiny bit liked, or a tiny bit disliked. You can have an *okay* day. People can want to be your friend but might not act friendly right away. The goal is to think "gray" and walk the middle path instead of relying on extreme ends of the spectrum.

Name the Speaker of Your Thoughts

Let's name the speaker of your unhelpful thoughts (or thought traps). What name do you want to create for your speaker? Mildred, Frank, Emily? When you notice a thought trap arise, I want you to greet it properly, with kindness and dignity. Respond to it. This may sound like, "Oh, hello, Mildred! Nice to see you again. Have a cup of tea, but I'm not going to chat."

As ridiculous as this sounds, naming the speaker of your thoughts will reduce its intensity. You may hear your unhelpful thoughts chatter in the background; however, resist the urge to be rude. That makes unhelpful thoughts louder. We also don't want to indulge them for hours or get deep into conversation. Aim for a simple and friendly acknowledgment, then move along. You can also jot down thoughts and check the facts. Remember, we want to acknowledge our thoughts as thoughts, not facts. With practice, your thought traps will become less influential.

CHALLENGING UNHELPFUL THOUGHTS

The first step in addressing unhelpful thought patterns is catching them when they occur. Getting angry with yourself for having certain thoughts is like getting angry at the ocean for making waves. So, don't stop, block, or get harsh with your thoughts. Notice the thoughts, greet them with friendliness, gently challenge them, and then redirect your attention.

I invite you to start noticing when you may be catastrophizing, mind reading, spotlighting, or going into all-or-nothing thinking patterns. In this section, we will talk about practical ways to address unhelpful thoughts. Identifying and then gently challenging our unhelpful thinking patterns can help us move through social interactions with less anxiety. The goal is to practice using these techniques so that we can socialize even when unhelpful thoughts are present. These thoughts may not go away completely, but they can change and feel a lot less disruptive.

CATASTROPHIZING

When you start catastrophizing, write down the best possible outcome, worst possible outcome, and most likely outcome. Humans tend to skew toward the negative. Many of us have what's called a negativity bias. Oftentimes, the worst-case scenario doesn't happen, and the most likely scenario does.

Let's say that you didn't get invited to a party. A catastrophic thought using the worst possible outcome might sound like, *They really, truly hate me*. The most likely outcome might sound like, *Maybe they want to get to know me better before inviting me*. The best-case scenario might sound like, *Maybe my invite is late*. Now it's your time to try it out! Write down the best, worst, and most likely outcomes based on a scenario.

Best

Most Likely

Worst

MIND READING

When you start mind reading, look for evidence and get curious. What evidence do you have to support your perception? If you feel that someone dislikes you, what is that based on? Practice being a detective. Get curious about the facts. What are the facts for and against your perception? Seek alternative viewpoints. You can build this detective skill by describing observations nonjudgmentally. Imagine a famous villain. Now, describe what that villain looks like. You might say things like, "mean, ugly, crazy-looking." However, those observations are biased. Now, describe that villain again, nonjudgmentally, based on what you actually see and not what you think. An example of this might sound like, "black-and-white hair, large eyes, sharp teeth, gray coat." As you can see, the first description is judgment-based, but the second description is fact-based. You can also ask clarifying questions to check the facts. This might sound like, "Are you mad at me?"

SPOTLIGHTING

When you feel that your every move is being examined, zoom out and put your thoughts into perspective. Turn your head from side to side and scan your environment. Notice people's reactions. You might notice how little other people are paying attention. Now zoom out further and focus your attention on the fact that you are one person in a school filled with hundreds of teens (who are all imperfect by the way). Zoom out further and realize the fact that you are one person in a community filled with thousands of people. Zoom out once more and notice the fact that you are one person out of millions of people in this country. When I experience spotlighting, it helps to picture myself standing in front of a huge mountain. Remembering how small we are helps change perspectives. In the broad scheme of things, will you remember a specific mistake five years from now, or even next month? Probably not.

ALL-OR-NOTHING THINKING

The world is filled with opposites, in-betweens, and gray areas. When you experience all-or-nothing thinking, search for the middle ground or gray area. This can also be referred to as walking the middle path. If you find yourself thinking words like *never*, *ever*, or *always*, that's a sign that you're practicing all-or-nothing-thinking. Try replacing these words with *sometimes*, *possibly*, and *maybe*. Instead of *I always get nervous*, reframe that thought as *I sometimes get nervous*. Instead of *I never want to try again*, reframe that thought as *Sometimes it's hard to find the motivation to try, and I will still try*. Instead of *No one ever listens to me*, reframe that thought as *Sometimes it feels like no one is listening.* Avoid picking a side. Even opposites can both be true at the same time. For example, you can feel brave and scared, confident and uncomfortable. You can be open and private. You can accept reality and change aspects of it.

OPPOSITE ACTION

Sometimes our unhelpful thoughts, or thought traps, generate intensified emotions and action urges (urges to do something). One example is feeling shame and consequently avoiding social contact because you *think* that one person doesn't like you. Opposite action is acting opposite of your emotion's action urge. Although all emotions are valid, and there's no "wrong" way to feel, this exercise helps you evaluate whether to act on certain emotions, thoughts, and action urges. If the emotion fits the facts, then problem solve and don't practice opposite action. For example, if you're being bullied, problem solve by asking for help from a trusted adult.

We only want to practice opposite action when our emotional intensity does not fit the facts or if acting on that urge would not be helpful. Let's say that a friend said they would text you after school, but they never did. As a result, you feel intense shame and have the urge to stay home from school. As painful (and valid) as your emotions are, it's not helping you in the long run to avoid school and isolate yourself in a shame spiral.

Prompt: Think of a scenario. Notice your thoughts, emotions, and action urges associated with it. Does your emotional intensity fit the facts? Is acting on it effective? If your action urge is problematic or doesn't fit the facts, practice opposite action. Read the examples and then fill in your own scenarios!

continued ›

THOUGHT	EMOTION	ACTION URGE	FITS THE FACTS + HELPFUL TO ACT ON URGE? (Y/N)	OPPOSITE ACTION (Y/N)
Ex: No one likes me.	*Sadness*	*Withdraw/ isolate*	*N*	**Y:** *Move your body, take a walk, get active, talk to someone*
Ex: If I fail this test, I'll never succeed.	*Fear*	*Avoid studying*	*N*	**Y:** *Approach studying in increments, break it down to small steps*
Ex: I'm scared of school because I'm being bullied.	*Fear and shame*	*Hide/avoid*	*Y*	**N:** *PROBLEM SOLVE: Tell an adult/ask for help*

THOUGHT	EMOTION	ACTION URGE	FITS THE FACTS + HELPFUL TO ACT ON URGE? (Y/N)	OPPOSITE ACTION (Y/N)

GIVE IT A TRY

It may not be fun to put yourself in social situations that increase anxiety. By practicing facing your anxiety triggers in digestible increments, you lower your anxiety in the long term. The opposite is also true: Avoiding anxiety triggers amplifies anxiety in the long term. There's pain that produces growth, and there's pain that just produces more pain. Avoiding creates more pain (most of the time), practicing skills reduces long-term pain. Everyone is worthy and capable of growth.

Thich Nhat Hanh, a Vietnamese Zen Buddhist spiritual leader, mentioned this topic of pain and growth using the analogy of the delicate white lotus flower that grows out of mud. He explained, "No mud, no lotus." In this way, beauty can emerge from certain types of pain. Without discomfort, there can't be comfort. Without sadness, there can be no happiness. We need both.

Following this train of thought, practicing skills and working through pain by challenging unhelpful thought patterns builds your ability to socialize with greater ease. Engaging in skills to manage anxiety can also reduce dependence on avoidance and safety behaviors in social situations. The more we practice pushing through moments of discomfort to socialize, the easier it will be to socialize. With practice, our anxiety will start to feel less intense. Please note that if discomfort turns into suffering and/or becomes prolonged, paralyzing, or all-encompassing, it's time to seek support from a counselor or therapist. Remember, seeking support for anxiety is no different than seeking support for a stomachache. (The stomach and brain are both body parts.) You are not a failure for needing support. It simply means that the available resources are not meeting your needs.

STEP-BY-STEP

Experiencing doses of manageable anxiety to avoid feeling randomly hijacked by anxiety is the goal here. When we put ourselves in situations that bring up anxiety and don't act on avoidance urges, we learn that socializing is safer than we thought. This is where approaching your anxiety comes in. Approaching your anxiety essentially means coming in contact with situations that increase anxiety (to break patterns of avoidance). It reduces long-term anxiety by giving you increments of manageable anxiety. Although I don't recommend performing therapy to approach your anxiety on yourself without the aid of a therapist, you can incorporate aspects of this technique into your life to help you overcome anxiety around socializing. There are different ways to practice approaching your anxiety, such as in-the-moment, imaginal, and body sensations. When successfully implemented, approaching your anxiety over time can teach you that you're capable of overcoming your fears, managing your anxiety, and reframing beliefs about your ability to socialize.

Imagine that you're tasked with climbing a ladder to achieve your goals. Skills and practices to approach your anxiety are the rungs in your ladder. Practices to approach your anxiety are anything that engages you to face a fear or anxiety. Each time you successfully push through urges to avoid anxiety, you climb upward. Some people may need more help than this book to climb their ladder, and that's okay! If you want help, if anxiety is more than an inconvenience, if you feel paralyzed by your anxiety, or if you avoid certain people, places, and situations to the point that it's negatively affecting your life, then you should talk to a therapist. We do not want to practice approaching things that pose a real threat; I'm not going to ask you to pet a wild bear. However, we do want to practice aspects of approaching your anxiety related to interactions that inhibit joy and connection. This is where approaching your anxiety related to socializing comes in. Most social interactions don't pose a real threat.

If approaching your anxiety in the moment is too intense for you, try first imagining the social interactions in your head. Play out a movie in your head and imagine how you want your interactions to go. Imagine the best-case scenario. In this way, you can build up to practicing approaching your anxiety in person. Just remember, unhelpful thoughts are not going to disappear. That's okay. Thoughts are allowed to visit, but they don't have to dictate our actions. Practicing approaching your anxiety helps us tolerate discomfort and develop new patterns relating to experiences.

For some readers, this may mean making eye contact, smiling at someone, or raising your hand. You can also practice approaching your anxiety by giving up just one safety behavior or modifying a safety behavior. Even reading about social skills can be effective in and of itself!

PREDICTIONS VERSUS REALITY

It's common to try and predict how the future might unfold. Many teens with anxiety often worry about future events. When we try to predict future outcomes, that's our way of compensating for the unknown. Yet again, a wonderful example of our mind trying to protect us. However, many of our future predictions have a negative bias rooted in fear of the unknown. As we know, our anxiety can cue both helpful and unhelpful interpretations and urges.

Let's make a note of how your predictions fared against the actual outcomes of what happened. When you practice experiencing social situations that stir up manageable doses of anxiety, did the outcome match your prediction? How about making eye contact? What was it like to raise your hand in class? Did the worst-case scenario happen? Again, if approaching your anxiety in person is too intense, practice imagining scenarios and tolerating your body sensations that arise. If your body sensations become too intense, shift your focus to a part of your body that feels comfortable and safe. Then, switch back to the uncomfortable sensation. Shifting to and from comfort and discomfort helps empower us. Successfully practicing and mastering approaching your anxiety recalibrates your internal alarm system. Over time, and with lots of repetition, you'll learn that practicing approaching your anxiety pays off. You'll also find that your outcomes weren't as bad as you predicted. Along the way, always make note of your wins.

Practicing approaching your anxiety is like taking swimming lessons. Each time we practice a stroke, our muscle memory becomes reinforced. Most people don't have to consciously tell their arms to move in order to swim. With practice, your body remembers. In the same way, with practice, your body will remember that it is safe to socialize. Some of us are natural swimmers. Maybe our ancestors swam every day. Thus, for some of us, swimming is easier to pick up. Others have to work a little harder to learn how to swim. That's okay. You have talents that others don't have. Again, practicing formal ways of approaching your anxiety is best when working with a mental health professional; however, you can try some takeaways from this section!

CHECKING YOUR THOUGHTS

Before practicing approaching your anxiety, rate your anxiety level about approaching a particular anxiety on a scale from 1 to 10. Unless you're working with a mental health professional, only practice approaching anxieties that bring up a level 5 anxiety or below. Anything above a 5 should be left for a therapy visit. Small successful practices are helpful. Unsuccessful practices can reinforce anxiety. Start small and simple.

When you're starting to practice approaching your anxiety, you may hear unhelpful thoughts and feel uncomfortable body sensations emerge. That's to be expected. When that happens, remember that you can still socialize with these thoughts and sensations. Here are some ways that you can tolerate discomfort and resist avoiding: Name the speaker of your thoughts, check the facts, practice opposite action, focus on a safe sensation within your body, or hum the phrase "Just because you think it, doesn't mean it's true." Humming activates something called our parasympathetic nervous system, which helps us self-soothe.

You can also ground yourself with things you can see, hear, smell, touch, and taste. For instance, you can put cold water on your face. Before approaching any anxiety, remind yourself why you're doing this in the first place. Try different ways of approaching your anxiety (imaginable, in the moment, or body sensation) to find what works for you.

Anxiety as Motivation

Anxiety is often misunderstood, especially among those who might see it as a negative emotion (and want to get rid of it). However, you don't need to get rid of your anxiety to socialize with more ease. Anxiety can be transformed into your superpower; your spidey-sense. By harnessing its energy, you can turn anxiety into a guide that pushes you forward or helps you pause. Rather than seeing anxiety as an obstacle, it's possible to view anxiety as our internal gauge, energy source, and advisor.

When you learn to manage and respond to your anxiety constructively, it can become a powerful motivator. This view of anxiety not only helps in reducing the negative impact of anxiety, it also enables us to use it as a driving force to achieve our goals. So how the heck can we get there? Great question. It starts with mindful awareness, curiosity, compassion, and balancing acceptance and change. We live in a change-based, improvement-powered world. You may be surrounded by messages that you need to look better, do better, try harder, strive more, and push yourself. But what about anti-hustle? What would it feel like to balance pushing yourself and resting? It's essential to be aware of two truths: that it is sometimes more helpful to push yourself, and sometimes more helpful to slow down, rest, and reset. While balancing these two truths, learning to observe anxiety and pause before reacting is a powerful tool that can transform anxiety into your ally.

PREDICTIONS VERSUS REAL OUTCOMES

Let's reflect on the difference between our predictions and real outcomes. In the boxes that follow, note examples of past social situations that stirred up some anxiety. Write down what you thought would happen in that social situation. What were you afraid of happening? This is the predicted outcome. Then, write down the real outcome, or what actually happened. You may notice that this is like the best case, worst case, and most likely scenario exercise. Read the example and fill in your own situations.

SITUATION	MY PREDICTION	WHAT HAPPENED WHEN I DIDN'T AVOID THE SITUATION
Ex: I was nervous about a big family party.	I felt like I would act awkward and not know what to say or say the wrong things.	I felt a little nervous, then smiled at a few people and said hello. I ended up having some nice conversations.

continued ›

Notice the difference between your predictions and what happened. You may want to pay attention to where your worry thoughts take you. How close or how far off were your predictions? If it's far off, this is an invitation to keep checking the facts. Just remember to experiment with the skills to find the skills that work best for you!

Reflection Questions

1. What's one in-the-moment way of approaching your anxiety that you are willing to try this week? (Ex: *I will say hello to my teacher.*)

____

____

____

2. Now imagine one scenario where you approach your anxiety instead of giving in to the impulse to avoid. (Ex: *I will imagine walking into the art room to finally join the art club.*)

____

____

____

3. What's one body sensation that you are willing to try tolerating this week? (Ex: *I can sit with my heart racing fast for thirty seconds.*)

____

____

____

Chapter 4

Showing Up as Your Best Self

It's important to embrace and show up as your authentic self. In this chapter, we will discuss everything from confidence to boundaries and mindset strategies so that you have the tools to make new friends, deepen existing friendships, and navigate any social situation with more ease. You'll learn practical ways to approach a variety of common social situations from a centered and confident place. I'll also share a custom recipe for making a delicious social skills cake. If you don't have a sweet tooth, replace this example with mac and cheese.

WHEN NO ONE UNDERSTANDS

No one understands Mei. After moving to New York from Seattle, Mei has trouble making new friends. She feels angry about having to start her life over in a new city. When a group of girls invites Mei to join them for lunch, Mei responds, "Just leave me alone." Mei doesn't *really* want to be left alone. She just feels self-conscious and angry and has difficulty setting boundaries without pushing others away. After months of interactions like this, Mei decides to pop into the school counselor's office. The counselor listens, and Mei feels understood. After a few sessions, Mei has a renewed sense of understanding. At lunch, even though her heart is beating fast and she feels nervous, she walks up to the same girls who once invited her to lunch. Mei asks if she can sit with them. They agree and welcome Mei to their table. Mei smiles before biting into her sandwich—she finally feels understood and accepted because she accepts herself a little more.

CONFIDENCE STARTS WITH YOUR MINDSET

Confidence is knowing that you are worthy. You are no better or worse than anyone else. Confidence is feeling secure in yourself and your abilities. It's the knowledge and felt sense that someone trusts and believes in themselves, without needing to prove anything. "Felt sense" loosely refers to body sensations that correlate to emotions or experiences. Confidence is not a fixed destination but a continuum with varying degrees on a spectrum. We can feel a little more or less confident at times. So, how do we create a more confident mindset?

We can't talk about confidence without talking about the "F" word: failure. Confidence is built when we take risks, try new things, and gain mastery over difficult experiences. It's inevitable that we will fail and struggle sometimes. Not everyone will like you—and that's okay! Struggle is a key ingredient for increasing confidence. How you interpret struggle is what matters. Failure is a vital piece of the confidence puzzle. I would even argue that confidence wouldn't exist without struggle and failure, so let's not avoid them. Here are some tips to boost your confidence and reframe your mindset.

Engage in activities that are a little hard but make you feel proud once you've accomplished them. Practice over and over. Reward yourself whenever you push through struggle. Notice your confidence levels in various situations. What makes you feel more or less confident? How does confidence feel in your body? To increase confidence, try a superhero stance. Stand tall and proud with your chin up, eyes forward, shoulders back, and hands at your waist. Notice how that posture feels. Practice adapting this stance when approaching new people. Own your greatness. When someone compliments you, don't make excuses. Practice saying "thank you" and simply accepting the compliment. Check yourself. Resist the urge to base your self-worth on the opinion of others. Remember, no one is liked by everyone. You can feel fulfilled and happy even if you're not friends with everyone.

TURN THE SPOTLIGHT AROUND AND ADJUST EXPECTATIONS

Feeling self-conscious is the worst. It affects how we show up. To increase self-confidence, we need to turn the spotlight around and adjust our expectations. I'll let you in on a little tip: You can show up as your "best" self, even if you're feeling self-conscious. Let me explain. Your best is going to look different each day. Your best is different at 6:00 a.m. versus 1:00 p.m., right? If you're feeling healthy, your best is going to look different than if you're feeling sick.

You define what your best looks like. We get into trouble when our expectations do not fit reality. With expectations in mind, when you're feeling self-conscious, focus outside yourself. Just because we think everyone is paying attention to us doesn't mean that they are. When you feel the spotlight is on you, ask yourself, "What can I learn about others?" Notice how others' voices change from quiet to loud. Notice what other people are wearing. Notice the sky outside. Focus your attention on how many colors you can name in the room. Notice as many external details as possible. When you focus on details, it helps ground you in the present moment and shifts your attention from your thoughts to facts and observations. Recognizing all of these other things in the universe makes less room for anxiety. When in doubt, adjust expectations and turn that spotlight around!

THE LIKE BUTTON

Comparisons aren't inherently bad. They inform us of where we are and where we want to be. Comparisons can be a vehicle for improvement and a measurement for progress. The downside is when we base our value on comparisons, or if comparisons leave us feeling helpless, jealous, or inadequate. In that event, comparisons are not helping and can keep us from trying new things and engaging with people. Here's how to reduce comparisons:

- Start by labeling when you're comparing yourself to others. "Oh, there I go again." Practice labeling again and again.
- Check the facts. You do not want to be a clone of your peers (trust me).
- Remember, no one can be good at everything. Some people will be better at certain things. Sometimes you will be better at certain things.
- Write three things that you are grateful for every day. Practicing gratitude is a proven technique based on plenty of research.
- Validate that everyone struggles. No one is perfect. What we see on the outside can be very different from what is on the inside. Even therapists can struggle. Perfection is not the goal. Living a full life is.
- Take a social media break. Set a realistic time frame (such as one to four hours) when you don't look at social media.

GROWTH MINDSET

A growth mindset is a belief in your ability to grow, change, and learn. The opposite of a growth mindset is called a fixed mindset. If you lean toward a fixed mindset, you believe that your failures are permanent or unchangeable. If you lean toward a growth mindset, you believe that your failures are temporary, and you can learn from your mistakes. These mindsets cause individuals to view challenges and setbacks differently. Teens with a growth mindset believe that they can get better with practice. A growth mindset can increase motivation, whereas a fixed mindset can decrease motivation.

If you have difficulty embracing a growth mindset, that's okay. It's not a matter of strength, will, or worthiness. Growth requires safety, nourishment, skills, and practice. Not all teens feel safe; reach out for support if all you can see are your failures or if you feel unsafe. Regardless of where you are, celebrating your hard work and efforts, no matter how little, can increase a growth mindset. Place emphasis on the steps that you take and the hard work that you put in, not always on the outcomes. Remember that you can grow with flaws and mistakes. Everyone in this universe makes mistakes and has flaws. There's a Japanese practice called *kintsugi*, which essentially means "to highlight imperfections." In this practice, cracked or broken pottery is enhanced and made stronger by filling the cracks with gold. Broken or imperfect objects are strengthened and beautified rather than thrown away. So, embrace your imperfections and grow with them!

DRAW YOURSELF AS A PLANT

Growth requires the right elements. A cactus needs different amounts of water and sunlight than a tulip does. If you treat a cactus like a tulip, it won't grow. Everyone's needs are different. What helps one person grow is not the same for every person. What do you need to grow?

Imagine yourself as a plant. What type of plant would you be? A rosebush, a cactus, a tree, a dandelion? Now draw yourself as a plant. Using the space provided, label three to five things that you need to grow. Examples of needs can be: *encouragement, sunlight, patience, persistence, rest, practice, connection, laughter, water, nourishing meals, hugs, breathing, trust, health, confidence, smiles, physical exercise*, etc.

Elements that I need to grow:

1. ______________________________

2. ______________________________

3. ______________________________

4. ______________________________

5. ______________________________

AUTHENTICALLY YOU

Authenticity means acting in a way that's aligned with your values and beliefs. Being authentic is being your full self, without hiding any aspects. It's expressing how you really feel, instead of how you think you should feel. It's being your true self, genuinely, openly, honestly, and radically. In this way, showing up authentically can help you develop meaningful connections (with yourself and others). Presenting your "true self" takes courage and clarity. Admittedly, it's difficult for some teens to expose their authentic selves when they are still figuring out who they are, what they want, what they like, and what they don't. You are likely in the process of forming your sense of self. There's still plenty of room for authenticity, even if you're questioning who you are. As humans, we are constantly evolving, changing, and growing based on our lived experiences so let's take some pressure off. If you don't feel that you are showing up authentically all the time, that's okay (and expected). The goal is not to be "perfectly authentic" 100 percent of the time. The goal is to check in with where you are on the authenticity spectrum. If you find yourself acting inauthentic, or "fake," that's a cue to swing back toward authenticity. Here are some pointers to help you show up as your authentic self:

- Develop expectations before social interactions. This may sound like, "Today, I'm not going to over-apologize," or "I'm not going to laugh at things that I don't think are actually funny," or "I'm not going to say that I like cheese when I really don't."
- Listen to your gut. If you get that "icky" feeling after an interaction where you acted out of character, that's your gut telling you that you're probably not acting authentically. That's an opportunity to act more authentic next time.
- Practice sharing your viewpoints and opinions. Often, we act inauthentic because we think others will not accept us. You may be surprised how people will still accept you, even when sharing unique quirks that make you, you!

Progressive Muscle Relaxation

Progressive muscle relaxation is the practice of tensing one muscle group at a time followed by relaxation and release of the tension. This exercise helps you release anxiety and tension from your body by relaxing your muscles.

- → Sit in a comfortable position.
- → Inhale while curling your toes and tightening your feet (as much as possible). Hold the tension, along with your breath, for ten seconds. Then, exhale dramatically through the mouth, releasing the tension and letting your feet quickly relax. Rest and breathe normally.
- → Inhale while tensing your thighs (as much as possible). Hold the tension, along with your breath, for ten seconds. Then, exhale dramatically through the mouth, releasing the tension from your thighs. Rest and breathe normally.
- → Inhale while tensing your fists (as much as possible). Hold the tension, along with your breath, for ten seconds. Then, exhale fully through the mouth, and quickly unfurl your hands. Rest and breathe normally.
- → Notice how your body feels.

SPEAKING UP

Let's break down what it means to communicate passively, aggressively, and assertively. I want you to imagine a long line, with passive on one end, aggressive on the other, and assertive in the middle.

Passive communication means that you put others' needs, opinions, and feelings before your own. In practice, this can sound like being overly apologetic, agreeing to everything, and pleasing others but ignoring your needs. A passive communicator may appear overly timid or quiet. Passivity can also look like doing favors for someone who never does favors for you. On the other hand, aggressive communicators bulldoze over the needs, opinions, or feelings of others. They tend to talk over others when communicating. In practice, this might look like raising your voice, interrupting, throwing your hands up, or making accusations. Aggressive communication is confrontational, argumentative, and tends to push others away.

Now let's talk about the middle ground, assertive communication. Assertive communication is expressing your needs, opinions, and feelings and also respecting the needs, opinions, and feelings of others. Assertiveness means clearly and directly establishing your values, without being pushy or unkind. You make room to listen to others and allow others to listen to you. Assertive communicators use "I" statements, maintain eye contact, and gently set boundaries. They say "no" when they don't want to do something. Assertive communication is direct but respectful and aims to understand all sides. Assertiveness is based on the belief that people are no better or worse than you. Learning to be an assertive communicator can help you reduce stress and increase respect from others.

EXPRESSING YOUR PREFERENCES

Letting others hear your voice is powerful. Everyone has different preferences, opinions, and ways of seeing the world. That's what makes life so interesting. If we all had the same viewpoints, life would be very boring. Inventions, discoveries, music, books, and art all exist because of different perspectives.

Communicating publicly, assertively, and honestly is not only good for you, but it's also good for others, too! Expressing your preferences allows others to connect with you and learn more about you. It's a way of processing information that can help you and other teens learn more effectively. Do you know why teachers ask you to work in groups? It's because teens learn from other teens, sometimes even more effectively than from teachers themselves. Sharing your opinions shows others that you are invested, engaged, and really care about a topic.

When you practice speaking up, you're killing two birds with one stone, since contributing your opinion can also be a goal and form of approaching your anxiety. If you push through the urge to stay quiet, you are once again creating new habits and ways of relating to your anxiety. When speaking up, start with topics that interest you. Start small by contributing a quick thought or anecdote.

SETTING BOUNDARIES

What does setting boundaries *really* mean? Let's get specific. Setting boundaries is a way of communicating your limits, needs, and values. Setting boundaries is a social skill that establishes ground rules for things that you are or aren't willing to do. The act of setting boundaries is not mean, rude, or aggressive. It's not a way of trying to control others. It's assertive. It's a healthy expression of your limits. Setting boundaries is a way to establish who you are, and what you do and don't stand for. Boundaries create safety and space.

Like any new social skill, it may be easier to test out setting a new boundary when you are feeling regulated (calm on the inside). Practice setting boundaries when you feel safe, centered, and somewhat confident. Avoid trying to set boundaries when you're upset, as it won't be as effective. Try practicing boundary setting with an assertive tone, not passive or aggressive. Look at the person, chin up, shoulders back, with a half smile.

You can practice with a pet first. This may sound like, "Ranger, I've asked you not to chew my sneakers." Body boundaries sound like, "I don't do hugs, I do high fives," or "I don't like to be touched, please do not touch my hair." If someone is talking badly about someone you like, emotional boundaries may sound like, "I don't think she's mean. I think she's a nice person. I like her." Time boundaries may sound like, "I'm not studying past 8:30 p.m. When I study past 8:30 p.m., I can't retain information."

SAYING "NO"

"No." One tiny word that can be so hard to express. Depending on your culture, gender expression, upbringing, and influences, you may have learned that expressing "no" is rude. Let's unpack these unhelpful perceptions. I challenge you to rethink your interpretation of "no." You can do this by seeing "no" for what it is. Remember, expressing "no" is not aggressive, rude, or inappropriate. "No" just simply means "no."

If you've experienced guilt after saying "no," remember that when you practice a new social skill, there will be a temporary increase in discomfort. However, feeling some discomfort doesn't mean that you should stop practicing—it means you should keep going. If you've experienced negative consequences after saying "no," let others know that you are practicing saying "no" or ask a trusted adult for help. Saying "no" protects your emotional, physical, and spiritual health. If we say "yes" to everything, we will be exposed to some pretty unsafe and unhealthy situations. Along with that, here are some phrases that you can try to practice your no's: "No, thank you, not today," "Let me think about it," "That doesn't make me feel comfortable," "I'm not sure," "Not for me," or "I think I'll pass."

PUTTING IT TO PRACTICE

Let's put this to practice. First, write down a date, time, and person with whom you are going to practice assertive communication, along with what you want to express. Ex: *On Saturday at noon, I'm going to tell Katie that I don't want to watch a horror movie.*

On ____________________ at ____________________ I'm going to tell

____________________ that ______________________________________

____.

Fill in the corresponding table with your own example. What would this statement look like if it were expressed passively, assertively, and aggressively? Finally, jump off the page and practice. Remember, eyes up, shoulders back, speak clearly.

SCENARIO	PASSIVE OPTION	ASSERTIVE OPTION	AGGRESSIVE OPTION
Ex: I don't want to watch a horror movie. I want to watch a comedy.	Stay quiet and watch a horror movie, even though I don't want to.	"I know you want to watch a horror movie, but I'm more into comedies these days. Can we compromise and see something else?"	"Why don't you understand? You should know that I don't like horror movies!"

TAKING FEEDBACK

Learning to take feedback without defensiveness is the Mount Everest of social skills! For some of us, feedback cues our anxiety. We can feel attacked even when no one is attacking us. We can go to great lengths to defend ourselves, make excuses, and explain (or overexplain) ourselves. I've been on both sides of this cycle.

Defensiveness is born out of insecurity. If we feel insecure and place our value in the hands of others, then feedback can devalue us. However, when we are secure in our value and worth, feedback doesn't hurt as much. Notice if you're catastrophizing or practicing all-or-nothing thinking in response to feedback. Be mindful of jumping to conclusions and leaning toward a negativity bias.

Let's practice ways to skillfully digest feedback. Here's what to do when someone is speaking to you in the moment. First, (and I know this sounds strange), practice listening to feedback with a soft belly. Place one hand on your belly and gently release any tension. Soften your belly (let it extend outward) and relax your jaw. Releasing tension in your jaw and belly makes you more relaxed and receptive to feedback. You can also try changing your posture and sit back, perhaps tenting your fingers by bringing the fingertips of each hand together to form a loose triangle shape. When taking feedback, nod your head, maintain eye contact, and resist the urge to interrupt or respond immediately. If there is a break in the feedback, feel free to offer, "Uh-huh. I see. I hear you." Pauses are great go-tos!

EMPATHY

Empathy is stepping into your friends' shoes and sensing their emotions. Empathy is the capacity to imagine what others may be feeling or needing. Empathetic actions are seedlings that blossom into closeness, friendship, and love. Expressing empathy is crucial to our well-being and socialization. It's the glue that holds our connections together. How intensely we experience people's emotions can vary. However, the goal of expressing empathy is not to be an emotional sponge; we don't want to soak up other people's worries. The goal is to convey that you hear, see, and support people.

People whose capacity for empathy happens to be heightened, may be "deep feelers" or empaths. If you're an empath, you can learn how to notice your emotional experiences so that you don't become completely overwhelmed or flooded by others' emotions. In this way, boundary skills and assertiveness might be particularly helpful. On the other side of the empathy spectrum, some teens need help learning how to show empathy. This is where empathetic body language might be particularly helpful. Regardless of where you land on the empathy spectrum, our thought patterns, behaviors, and ways of learning can look different. That's okay. Either way, approaching social situations with empathy eases anxiety by harnessing the power of this deep connection tool.

I'd argue that empathy is about 20 percent what you say and 80 percent how you say it (and if you genuinely "feel" it). You can express empathy through looks of concern, head nods, furrowing your brow, or placing your hand on your heart. Verbally expressing empathy sounds like speaking with inflection and passion. A statement may sound like, "I'm so sorry to hear that you broke your leg. That sounds horrible!" Bottom line, when expressing empathy, it's important that you communicate that you hear, see, and relate to others' experiences, even if you haven't experienced what they've been through.

COMPASSION

Compassion refers to the ability to sense others' emotions, paired with the desire to help. Compassion starts with empathy and takes it a little further. Compassion is action-oriented. Research shows that when we feel compassion, oxytocin, our "bonding hormone," is released. In the same way, our heart rate slows, preparing us to approach and soothe (the opposite of the fight, flight, or freeze impulse). If we are harsh and judgmental with ourselves, we will be harsh and judgmental toward others and push them away. When navigating social situations, practicing compassionate communication is a win-win situation because you're helping others and practicing self-kindness, too.

You can practice compassionate communication in social situations by using phrases such as "What can I do to help you?" "I'd like to visit you," or "I'll bring you your homework and make you hot chocolate." Nonverbally, this looks like saving a seat for someone, leaving a note in someone's locker, or sending them a text. With body language, and with permission, this may look like giving a person a hug or patting their back. Adopting a compassionate framework is good for your health. Practicing self-compassion is a pathway to practicing compassion for others. If we practice responding to our tough moments with a compassionate tone, this will help us gain the capacity to project this same compassion outward. Just remember, it starts with you and being tender, loving, and patient with yourself, especially in difficult moments. This is proven in the work of self-compassion experts, such as Dr. Kristin Neff, who demonstrates that practicing compassion predicts lower levels of anxiety and depression.

Reflection Questions

1. What's one thing that you have learned in this chapter?

2. What's one way that you can practice assertive communication while setting boundaries?

3. What does practicing empathy and compassion mean to you?

Chapter 5

Let's Talk about Talking

In this chapter, we'll cover helpful talking tips for various social scenarios. Remember, you can always customize these techniques to make them your own. My intention here is to plant seeds. You have the power to take these seeds and plant your own flowers. More than anything else, remember to practice these skills with authenticity, highlighting your own unique qualities. We will also review what to do when we fail at communicating effectively. Remember that failure is not bad. I'll give you pointers on how to get back up when you fail. After all, we are always learning (myself included).

WARM-UP TIME

It's the first day of summer camp. Ella is excited but also nervous about meeting her peers. Her heart pounds as she arrives at drop-off. During orientation, she's quiet. Everyone seems nice, but she stays in the background, avoiding eye contact. As the day goes on, Ella observes her peers kayaking on the clear blue lake. A moment of peace emerges, allowing for a soft belly breath. She starts to feel a little more comfortable. During craft time, Ella grabs a seat next to a girl who looks friendly. She takes another deep breath while beading a colorful necklace. Ella then turns to the girl and says, "I like your shoes. I'm Ella, by the way." The girl smiles back and introduces herself. They end up having a great conversation. Ella learns that they have a lot in common and feels happy inside. Ella knows that she just needs a little warm-up time to connect with others.

TALKING TIPS

You will do almost anything to avoid starting a conversation. You have things to say, but that lump in your throat makes it hard to speak up. Let's face it, socializing can feel overwhelming. Maybe your family has trouble understanding why you feel so shy. Maybe you do, too. If you find yourself rehearsing what you're going to say, or avoid speaking to people, you may be experiencing social anxiety. Here's the good news (and what I wish I knew as a teen): This is not a window into the future. Socializing can feel less painful. There are practices and tools to help you ease into conversations. How do I know? Well, because I've been there, too. You can learn how to socialize without constantly second-guessing yourself. Believe it or not, the world wants to hear from you, and you deserve to be heard.

MAKING INTRODUCTIONS

When introducing yourself, here are some tips. First, allow yourself some warm-up time. Then, approach people who appear friendly to you. You can also start by introducing yourself to people who you have something in common with. Another approach is to try small talk before you introduce yourself. In Ella's case, she started with a compliment, which can be an effective way to ease into an introduction. When introducing yourself, make eye contact, smile (or half smile), and find your own unique voice that feels right for you. This can sound like, "Hey, I'm Dashawn, by the way," or "Hey, I know we have some classes together. I'm not sure if we've met," or "I love your shirt; I have the same one," or you can start by asking the person's name. This may sound like, "I'm not sure if we've met. I'm Ella. What's your name?"

STARTING A CONVERSATION

Starting conversations can be intimidating. Here are some tips for starting conversations that make it easier.

Observe. Start a conversation by expressing something that you notice about a person. Example: "Hey, I like your shirt."

Start with a smile. Why? Because smiling conveys friendliness and openness. Smiling also generates positive emotions and raises your mood.

Look for common interests. Start a conversation with people who share your interests. Maybe you both like manga, cooking, or sports. Example: "Hey, did you watch that cooking show last night?"

Socialize around an activity. Initiate a conversation when you're playing basketball, taking an art class, or playing video games. Sometimes, it's easier to initiate conversations when we're physically active and moving. And when we're engaged in an activity, it can take the pressure off of needing to maintain eye contact.

Start small. "Good morning" can go a long way. Small phrases can be huge wins. If your long-term goal is to have meaningful conversations, it's helpful to start with small, manageable steps.

Start easy. Initiate conversations with the least intimidating people first. This could be a friend, school bus driver, mail carrier, librarian, or family member.

SWITCHING GEARS

Just because a person doesn't seem interested in chatting doesn't mean that they're not interested in you, or that they dislike you. It probably means one of the following:

1. They don't relate to the topic you're speaking about.
2. They need you to communicate differently.
3. It's not a good time for them to chat.

Instead of shutting down when someone doesn't respond, try switching gears. Ask clarifying questions or try out a different topic.

Here's a scenario to illustrate this in action:

"Hey, Kareem, did you see that football game last night?" Lauren asks.

"No." Kareem bluntly responds.

"Do you like football, or a different sport?" asks Lauren.

"Basketball is my jam. Did you see the Lakers play last night?"

In this example, Lauren switches gears and looks for a common interest. Kareem is more interested in basketball and wants to talk about that instead. Asking questions is a great way of learning and engaging in conversations.

SMALL TALK

Small talk is a great way to ease into conversations. When practicing small talk, start with an observation based on something you have in common with another person. Maybe you're in the same class, ride the bus together, or play the same video games or sports. This may sound like, "Hey, I think we share history class together, right?" Small talk can also be in the form of a compliment (who doesn't love compliments?). When practicing this, ask open-ended questions, actively listen to responses, and most of all, put away your phone. To keep the conversations going, show interest and enthusiasm in what they are saying. Remain curious.

Phrases may sound like, "Hmm, really?" or "Oh, that's interesting," or "Wow, I never knew that." Ask open-ended questions instead of close-ended questions (such as questions that prompt a yes or no answer). For example, instead of saying, "Did you do anything this weekend?" try saying, "What did you do this weekend?" See the difference? Open-ended questions start with the words "what" or "how." Bottom line, small talk can be easy for some and difficult for others. That's okay. We are here to find our unique way of communicating. The more we experiment with different ways of socializing, the more we can learn what works for us.

ACCEPTING AND GIVING COMPLIMENTS

It can feel uncomfortable to give and receive compliments sometimes. However, this social skill makes a big impact on relationships. When someone gives you a compliment, maintain eye contact, smile, and say "thank you." I know that seems basic, but we often have trouble doing it. Resist the urge to minimize your accomplishments. Avoid responding to compliments with phrases like, "Oh no, I didn't do much." Own your compliments. When giving compliments, start with specifics. Instead of "Your clothes are really cool," try "I really like your *Star Wars* shirt." Instead of "You're really smart," try "You're really good at math. You always have the answers in class." In this way, compliments can act as conversation openers. The more specific we are, the more doors will be open. Giving and accepting compliments communicates friendliness and makes others feel good about themselves. Thus, this is a helpful way to boost conversations!

BODY LANGUAGE AND PACE

Our body language and the pace at which we speak influence our communication skills. How we present ourselves when we're socializing really matters. If someone approaches you with their eyes down and arms crossed, what would you think? Not too approachable, right? If that same person approaches you with their head up and arms relaxed, what would you think? More friendly, right? The key to friendly body language is to keep your eyes up, shoulders back, arms uncrossed, hands relaxed. Now let's turn to the pace in which we speak. When we're nervous, sometimes we speak quickly. When this happens, it's hard for others to understand us. Try speaking a little slower. If others often say things like: "What?", "Can you repeat that?", or "Can you slow it down?", slow down your pace. Experiment with your body language and the pace at which you speak. See what happens!

MOVING THROUGH SOCIAL STRESS WITH A HUG

To communicate effectively with others, we need to feel safe in our bodies first. For people with anxiety around socializing, approaching others can be extremely stressful. Even though your feelings are valid, I promise you that socializing doesn't always have to be this hard. Here's a simple exercise to help you self-soothe and contain difficult or intense emotions around socializing. This exercise works by calming the nervous system and was developed by Dr. Peter Levine. You can practice this before social interactions.

1. Hug yourself by placing your right hand under your left armpit. Grab the side of your body. Place your left hand over the upper part of the opposite arm. Hold tightly for about two minutes.

2. As you're hugging yourself, pay attention to the sensations in your body.

3. Let yourself settle into this self-hug, allowing yourself to feel supported and contained by it.

4. Notice if there are any shifts with your breathing, body sensations, and perceptions of yourself.

Hopefully you feel less stressed, more grounded, and more connected to your body. You may also feel a little more emotionally safe and secure.

4-7-8 Breath

The 4-7-8 breath is an effective breathing technique based on an ancient yoga practice of controlling your breath. We may not be able to control our anxiety triggers, but we can almost always control our breathing. This breathing technique was developed by Dr. Andrew Weil and works by interrupting our stress response and increasing a sense of relaxation. Like all new skills, it works best when practiced daily.

Start by closing your mouth and gently placing your tongue behind your two front teeth.

Now inhale through your nose for four counts.
1 . . . 2 . . . 3 . . . 4.

Hold your breath for seven counts.
1 . . . 2 . . . 3 . . . 4 . . . 5 . . . 6 . . . 7.

Exhale completely through your mouth for eight counts. 1 . . . 2 . . . 3 . . . 4 . . . 5 . . . 6 . . . 7 . . . 8.
It may be helpful to make a "woosh" sound on the exhale.

On the exhale, imagine releasing stress, anxiety, or any tension that you may be holding.

Repeat the 4-7-8 breath pattern three to five times.

WHAT IF IT GOES WRONG?

Sometimes, things don't go exactly as planned. When it comes to socializing, we all make mistakes. That's okay, and even expected. No one is perfect. Even world leaders, top executives, and successful artists make mistakes, offend others, and act in a way that is not always aligned with their values. It's impossible to say the right things and act the right way 100 percent of the time. We're not robots, after all. In this section, we'll discuss how to approach setbacks.

When we don't show up as our best selves, or mess up, we can learn helpful techniques to respond skillfully. Often, it pains us when we mess up. This can show up as guilt, shame, or embarrassment. However, we have the option of making more pain in response to that initial pain, or not. When we judge ourselves for our mistakes, that adds more pain. When we're understanding, compassionate, and forgive ourselves, that reduces pain.

FORGIVING YOURSELF

Forgiveness can reduce blood pressure, anxiety levels, and even physical pain. Forgiveness is the decision to release feelings of anger, resentment, or vengeance at someone who has harmed you, regardless of whether they deserve to be forgiven.

Forgiveness is not denying, forgetting, or excusing hurt. It doesn't mean that you have to repair a relationship with the person who harmed you or erase accountability. Instead, forgiveness brings you peace of mind because you are choosing to let go of painful feelings stored within your mind and body.

If we can't forgive ourselves, we're going to have trouble forgiving others. To practice forgiveness, start by naming your hurt (for example, anger or sadness). Then, allow yourself to fully feel your hurt for one minute. Sit with your pain. Validate your pain—it's okay to feel hurt. Write about your pain through journaling. Finally, write a letter to the person who hurt you (or to yourself), using compassionate words. You don't have to send the letter. If you're having trouble letting go, that's okay. See if you can be loving toward yourself in moments of pain. Unclench your jaw and soften your body. Take a slow, soft belly breath. This may help with the process of beginning to work through the hurt instead of fighting it.

THE REPAIR

When we hurt someone, it's important to apologize and then repair. How we apologize and repair a situation often leaves more of a lasting impression than the mistake itself. When apologizing, avoid making excuses or blaming. An apology isn't "I'm sorry that you're feeling hurt, but you got me mad." An apology is "I'm sorry that I hurt your feelings. I will work on being kinder when I'm mad." See the difference? The first example places the blame on the other person, but the second example accepts responsibility. On the other hand, using an example of accidentally mispronouncing someone's name, over-apologizing might sound like, "OMG, I am so, so sorry. I can't believe that I did that. I will do anything if you can just please forgive me." This dialogue might be appropriate if you caused physical harm to someone, but not if you just accidentally mispronounced their name. Thus, try and make your repair balanced and appropriate in the context of the mistake.

THE CHECK-IN

When you mess up, after you've had time to recover, check in with yourself by asking yourself these questions:

1. *What do I need to have better interactions?* Examples might include rest, relaxation, confidence, or peers who share my interests.

2. *How did I feel during the interaction?* Examples might include happy, sad, ashamed, angry, or scared.

3. *If I had a do-over, what would I do slightly differently?* Possible revisions to your actions might include speaking more slowly or listening carefully.

Check-ins are not the same as something called rumination, or thought loops. We'll talk more about rumination in the next section. Check-ins are a way to nonjudgmentally evaluate what went wrong so that you can troubleshoot how to show up more authentically next time. They are proactive balanced reflections, not biased interpretations or opportunities for self-loathing. Check-ins allow us to acknowledge our humanness and figure out how to remove obstacles.

IF, THEN, AND

When social situations go wrong, here's what you can do to recover. Whether you've accidentally offended someone, or someone didn't respond well to your joke, there's always a way to recoup. After setbacks happen, worry thoughts can occur, "What if they don't like me?" This exercise helps you process anxiety around socializing and gives you tools to frame how to cope ahead next time.

For this exercise, I want you to follow your worry thoughts all the way through. Don't stop at "what if." Always add the words, "if, then, and" to worry thoughts. When filling in your "if, then, and" statements, experiment with using best-case, most-likely, and even worst-case scenarios. Practice "if, then, and" statements as many times as possible in your everyday life. With practice, you will notice a shift in your mindset.

Example: ***If*** *I offend someone with my words,* ***then*** *I will apologize* ***and*** *move on.*

Example: ***If*** *they laugh at me,* ***then*** *I will look for other people to socialize with* ***and*** *that will make me feel better.*

Now it's your turn:

If ______________________________, then ______________________________

and ______________________________

If ______________________________, then ______________________________

and ______________________________

If ______________________________, then ______________________________

and ______________________________

If ______________________________, then ______________________________

and ______________________________

If ______________________________, then ______________________________

and ______________________________

If ______________________________, then ______________________________

and ______________________________

If ______________________________, then ______________________________

and ______________________________

If ______________________________, then ______________________________

and ______________________________

If ______________________________, then ______________________________

and ______________________________

If ______________________________, then ______________________________

and ______________________________

If ______________________________, then ______________________________

and ______________________________

If ______________________________, then ______________________________

and ______________________________

WHAT I SHOULD HAVE SAID . . .

Let's dive into rumination. Rumination is repeated thinking about an idea, situation, or choice. Most of us get stuck on thoughts sometimes. However, rumination is when thoughts seem to be "stuck" on a never-ending loop. Rumination is your body's way of preparing (or over-preparing) you to do something. You may experience temporary relief after ruminating; however, that relief will be short-lived. When we are unnecessarily overprepared, our anxiety increases. In this way, anxiety loops can mirror rumination loops. Rumination also makes it difficult to develop connections because it's hard to be fully present if we're mulling over what happened ten minutes ago.

Humans have a constant stream of consciousness (or thoughts) flowing in and out. To address rumination, we have to start noticing which thoughts to "catch," which ones to ignore, and which ones to gently let go of. Here's how we can effectively respond to rumination. First, recognize the difference between having a thought and thinking. Thoughts are often out of our control. They come and go and are more unconscious. Thinking is actively paying attention to certain thoughts and is a more conscious act. Using the analogy of fishing, sometimes thoughts (like fish) come to the surface, or swim on by. With a fishing rod (our attention), we can choose what fish (or thoughts) to "catch" (or pay attention to). We can also choose what thoughts to let go of; you can even decide not to catch any fish at all.

When rumination occurs, label thoughts as thoughts, not facts. Then ask yourself if the thought is worth exploring. Remember to resist the urge to block thoughts (that makes rumination worse). Instead, observe the thought, make room for it for five minutes, and then shift your attention away from your thoughts by reanchoring yourself in your surroundings. You can do this by engaging your five senses. Touch something soft, smell something pleasant, taste something tart or juicy, listen to music, look at images of nature or animals, move your body, take a walk—ground yourself in the present moment and in your sensations.

Reflection Questions

1. What's one thing that you learned in this chapter?

2. What's one skill that you can practice when you make a mistake?

3. What are two strengths that you have in regard to socializing? (Examples can include: I'm funny, I'm kind, I'm generous, I care, I'm different, I'm interesting, I'm creative, I'm smart.)

Chapter 6

Using Your Body Language (and Your Ears!)

Your body is wise. If you listen carefully, it can help you form a deep understanding of yourself and others. That's why, in this chapter, we'll explore everything from eye contact to hand gestures to active listening. Just remember, people only hear a very small percentage of what you actually say; they are more likely to remember how you made them feel. This is where body language comes in. Since our minds and bodies are in constant communication, how we communicate with our bodies is key to growing authentic connections. Learning to be more embodied (or connected to our bodies) helps us relate to ourselves and the world around us.

DRAWING PEOPLE IN

Juan is funny and smart. He can list off any fact about baseball and has won more video games than any of his peers. However, Juan has trouble socializing. Juan often feels disconnected from his body. He has trouble knowing when he's hungry, thirsty, or cold. He also has trouble reading the body language of others. Juan gets a little too close when he socializes with his peers. He rarely smiles and usually looks at the ground when speaking. As a result, Juan pushes people away. He feels lonely and just wants to be liked. His attempts to emotionally connect to his peers frequently backfire. He's frustrated and thinks that no one likes him. Here's what I want to tell Juan: It's not that your peers don't like you. It's more likely that you just need to practice effective nonverbal communication strategies to draw people in—not push them away!

NONVERBAL COMMUNICATION TIPS

Before we explore nonverbal communication tips, we first need to understand why it's so important to listen to our bodies. Did you know that anxiety can literally throw your physical body off balance? Stress and anxiety can elevate hormones like cortisol, which can impact your vestibular system (your body's internal balance control system). That may be why anxiety can make us feel dizzy. Noticing how you are feeling in your body (sensations and emotions) can help you reconnect, shift your thinking, and rebalance. We count on body sensations to let us know if we're too hot, cold, hungry, tired, thirsty, angry, sick, or in danger. This is also called interoception. Increased awareness of your body sensations is linked to well-being and emotion regulation. If you mistake thirst for hunger, you will overeat. If you mistake fatigue for anxiety, you will feel exhausted. If you mistake excitement for anger, people will have trouble understanding your reactions.

If we cannot notice, tolerate, and respond to our own body sensations, then how are we supposed to notice, tolerate, and respond to others? The nonverbal communication tips that follow will be geared toward self-awareness practices and exercises to use with others. Before we proceed, keep in mind that, although we want to increase self-awareness, we don't want to increase spotlighting or overanalyze our every thought and body sensation. Experiment with finding your middle ground. Too much emphasis on increasing body awareness can feel overwhelming, so go slow and listen to your limits and body cues. You are in control here!

EYE CONTACT

Try a soft eye gaze. This means letting your eyes relax and your eyelids droop just a little bit as you look at something or someone. A soft gaze is the act of looking as if you were gazing at the ocean or a beloved pet. The opposite of a soft gaze is looking startled with your eyes wide open. Practice a soft gaze throughout the day in a mirror, then try it outside. Make eye contact with people far away from you at first. You can also practice making eye contact with people you don't find intimidating. Notice what that feels like. Once that becomes easier, practice looking at people while they are speaking to you. Start with a few seconds at a time, slowly increasing the time. If you ever feel overwhelmed, you can always gently shift your gaze to their ear or forehead for a second, then shift back to their eyes. It's okay to give yourself a break with eye contact; just remember to come back to it.

POSTURE

How we carry our bodies communicates a lot both internally and externally. Let's say a dog approaches you with its eyes locked on yours, head lowered, teeth bared, and body tense. What would you think? Now let's say another dog approaches you wagging its tail, tongue out, head up. In this way, we are not very different from dogs. When you put your shoulders back, lift your gaze, and half smile, you communicate confidence and friendliness. Alternatively, if you're hunched over with your head down, that communicates insecurity. Try committing to two posture changes this week. You don't have to embrace them all. If you could pick any two of these, which ones do you want to try? Here are your options:

- Half smile (gently upturn the corners of your mouth)
- Shoulders back
- Eyes up
- Chin up
- Adjust closeness according to others' body language; if they step back, that means that they need more personal space
- Relaxed, open hands (avoid closed arms and fists)
- Listen with a soft belly

FACIAL EXPRESSIONS

Humans are biologically designed to study and interpret facial expressions—our survival depends on it. Facial expressions are a vital part of social interactions because these expressions alert us to how a person is feeling and how they are perceiving us. They tell us if someone is scared, calm, sad, or angry. These signals are converted into how we behave in relation to them. When we're tense, our face will tense. When we're relaxed, our face will relax. With a mirror, play around with different facial expressions. What do these facial expressions feel like and look like? What does each facial expression communicate to others? Match your facial expression to what you want to express; if it doesn't match, others may be confused. Try out these expressions:

- Tense your face by pushing your eyebrows together and squinting your eyes
- Relax your face; try a soft gaze and a half smile
- Practice facial expressions of happiness, sadness, fear, anger, surprise, and disgust

HAND GESTURES

Do you cross your arms a lot? When I was a teen, I did this when I was feeling nervous in social situations. Crossing your arms and covering your hands is a protective gesture. Therefore, when you hide your hands, that can communicate that you're not open to socializing. When humans are being honest, they tend to expose the palms of their hands. Car salespeople sometimes look for this cue to tell if a person really wants to buy a car or not. Likewise, if you've ever watched politicians on TV, you'll see that they often have their hands exposed, palms open, facing up. This signals openness and honesty. Here are some takeaways for hand gestures that invite people in. Try them out and notice how each hand gesture feels:

- Expose your hands. Resist the urge to hide them.
- Relax and open your hands.
- Extend your hands outward toward others.
- Increase confidence by loosely intertwining your hands and placing them on a table.

PERSONAL DISTANCE

Personal distance varies depending on our culture, upbringing, and life experiences. There's no "right" formula, but here are some helpful guidelines to figure out what feels right for you and others. Personal distance varies from person to person. You'd probably give your teacher more personal space than a loved one, right? Let's view personal distance in the context of the social situation.

The first step is to observe the social situation. Notice how close others are to one another. Try to match what seems socially appropriate based on what you observe. If you feel uncomfortable, that's a sign that someone might be too close. If someone backs away or leans away from you when you're speaking, that means that you're too close to them. In this case, take a step back. Everyone gets to decide the amount of personal space that feels right for them.

EMOTIONAL POSES

Let's practice embodying different emotions! Try out this exercise in a safe space, like your bedroom. Act out each emotion using only your body language and facial expressions. Hold each pose for at least one minute. Try your best to exaggerate each emotion using just your body and making no sound. This exercise helps increase emotional intelligence and insight into emotions and body language. You may also notice which emotions you tend to embody most often. After you go through all the poses, take a few moments to answer the questions that follow. If you prefer, you can also draw what these emotions look like, too!

Act out the following five emotions. Hold each pose for one minute:

1. Anger
2. Sadness
3. Happiness
4. Surprise
5. Fear

Which emotion feels the most familiar or safe to you?

___

Which emotion feels the most foreign or uncomfortable to you?

___

Which emotion do you want to embody more often?

___

READING BODY LANGUAGE

Reading body language involves understanding an array of nonverbal cues, such as body movements, facial expressions, and gestures. Reading these cues is an important part of socialization since they can help us navigate our behaviors in social situations. Body language also helps us understand how people are feeling. Just remember: People pay more attention to people's body language than their words. Case in point, if a person yawns in the middle of a conversation, that gesture probably communicates that they're tired or not interested in what you're saying. Here are six tips to help you read the body language of others.

Observe how others are standing. If their feet are facing toward you, that could mean that they are interested in socializing. If their feet are facing away, that could indicate that it's not a good time to spark conversation.

Look for invitations to socialize. Invitations might be a smile, open hands, laughter, open body language, or eye contact.

See if others are mirroring you. Mirroring basically means mimicking another person's body language. It's usually unconscious—we do it without even thinking. If a person is mirroring you, that's another invitation to socialize.

Notice people's facial expressions. If they don't seem to have any facial expression or look bored, that's a cue to reevaluate socializing with them at that moment. Remember, it's not that they necessarily don't like you; it just might not be a good time to socialize.

Notice people's proximity to you. If they move away from you when you are trying to communicate, that's a sign to back away and give them more personal space.

Notice the way others position their heads. Are they nodding along, listening to what you're saying, or maybe tilting their head to the side? That's a sign that someone is listening to what you're saying.

Using Your Imagination to Relieve Anxiety

Anxiety can make us feel unsafe. This tip helps you regain a sense of safety when you're feeling anxious. Imagine a safe place. It can be real or imaginary, ordinary or extraordinary. Your safe place can be somewhere you have been or somewhere you want to go. Take a moment to transport yourself to this safe place. Imagine being there.

What are you doing in your safe place? Are you lying down, walking, sitting, standing, or swimming? Notice the temperature, smells, colors, and sounds. Is it warm or cool, windy or still? Is there anyone with you or are you alone? Notice how your mind and body feel in this place. Before you leave your safe place, take a mental picture and store it somewhere safe within your body. Return to the image of your safe place whenever you need it. It may also help to create a drawing or collage of your safe place.

ALL EARS

Hearing is one of the first senses that we are born with. We can hear our mother's voice when we are inside the womb. Therefore, when someone deeply listens to you, you can feel understood, accepted, and even loved. Learning to be a deep listener is vital to our connections and well-being—it can literally help grow your brain and help you bond with others. There's evidence to suggest that listening can help increase connections of neurons in the brain throughout our life.

Active listening, or deep listening, means listening with your full awareness and attention, nonjudgmentally. No phones, no multitasking, no judgments. It means showing up fully present for someone, really hearing what they're saying, and not just hearing what you think they are saying. It means resisting the urge to interpret or jump to conclusions. This way of listening can also be referred to as "beginner's ear," or hearing with curiosity. We'll be reviewing four different active listening strategies to help you become a deep, active, and mindful listener!

AVOID INTERRUPTIONS

When we interrupt, we're sending the message that what we have to say is more important than what others have to say. So why do we interrupt? Sometimes people's words trigger emotions that are difficult to tolerate. If we can't tolerate or regulate our own emotions, we'll be more likely to interrupt! Interrupting is kind of like an avoidance strategy. We want to grow connections, not avoidance. Here are some tips to avoid interruptions:

Talk less. It may seem obvious, but practice taking a step back in conversations to allow others to be heard.

Notice your urge to interrupt and label it. "Oh, there it is again, that urge to interrupt."

Ground yourself in your breath. Practice deep belly breathing to regulate your emotions when you have an urge to interrupt.

Relax your belly. A soft belly allows us to listen more effectively.

SHOW THAT YOU'RE LISTENING

It takes effort to show that you're deeply listening. We tend to become distracted by an endless list of to-dos, notifications, texts, calls, thoughts, emails, etc. The more we practice multitasking, the harder it will be to listen. Therefore, our capacity for listening mirrors our attention capacity. The more we practice focusing our attention, the easier it will be to deeply listen. If you're wondering why it may feel so exhausting to actively listen, it may be because your attention capacity is low. Likewise, it's also hard to listen if you feel stressed or anxious. However, let's make room to honor your starting point. Here are some tips to help you increase your listening capacity!

- Ask yourself, "Is this a good time for me to listen?" If the answer is no, then kindly ask the person if you could have a few minutes (or hours) to recalibrate your attention capacity.
- Take soft belly breaths and listen with a soft belly. When we are relaxed, our parasympathetic nervous system is engaged and we have the resources to actually listen.
- Put your phone away and focus your attention on the person speaking.
- Look at the person in the eyes with "soft eyes" (see page 91).
- Slowly nod along.
- Mirror their facial expressions or body language.
- Wait for the other person to stop talking before responding.
- Focus your attention on their tone, pitch, and the way that they speak from a curious lens.

DON'T PRE-FORM YOUR REPLY

When we pre-form replies, it takes us out of the present moment. Sometimes we rehearse or pre-form replies out of fear of not saying the "right" thing. However, as we know, the worst-case scenario is not very likely to happen. Your reply doesn't have to be perfect, but it will help if it's authentic. Rehearsed replies sometimes don't resonate with others, as those responses can feel prefabricated or ingenuine. Authentic responses require pause, deliberation, and thoughtfulness. When you notice yourself rehearsing your response, here are some tips to try out:

- Take a deep breath and refocus your attention on the person's face: Look at their eyebrows, eyes, or nose.
- Allow for pauses; you're allowed to pause before responding.
- If you don't know how to respond, just respond by validating. Examples of this may sound like "That sounds hard," or "I know you're going through a lot."
- Ride the urge to form replies instead of acting on it.

ASK QUESTIONS

Asking questions shows that you're interested and following along. When asking questions, the goal is to be a listener, not a fixer. It's okay, we all sometimes experience an urge to fix and problem solve. However, sometimes we just need friends to hear us out and inquire with a few questions. A way that you can practice listening is to ask questions. Keep in mind that you might not receive clear answers to your questions. However, that doesn't mean that the questions weren't helpful. If the person doesn't answer your questions, that's okay. The point is to demonstrate thoughtfulness and investment in conversations. Start with these questions:

- Recap what you are hearing, followed by a question: "I'm hearing that you got a bad grade, and you are super upset; is that right?"
- Can you tell me a little more?
- What's that like for you?
- What are you needing right now to feel better?

ACTIVE LISTENING

Below is an active listening practice that only takes about three minutes. You'll need a music source and a pen. After the practice, answer the following questions and jot down any notes you have:

1. Sit in a comfortable position. Limit distractions by shutting doors and turning off/putting away unnecessary devices.

2. On your computer, phone, or a radio, find a song in another language that you are not fluent in and that you've never heard before.

3. Once you've found the song, close your eyes or lower your gaze to the ground.

4. Press play and devote your full attention and awareness just to listening. Get *really curious*. Observe all the sounds, words, beats, and rhythms. Resist the urge to do anything else.

5. When the song is over, lift your gaze, and answer the following questions.

Questions:

What do you notice about that experience of active listening?

____

What do you think the song is about?

____

Reflection Questions

1. What does it feel like to actively listen versus "half" listen?

2. What's one nonverbal communication tip that you can practice this week?

3. Whether it's active listening or body language cues, can you name a skill that comes naturally to you? (For example: *personal distance, eye contact, reading body language, listening.*)

Chapter 7

Putting It into Practice

Learning to have a different relationship with anxiety is full of ups and downs, and mistakes and successes. That's expected. With that in mind, in this chapter, we will review everything from how to skillfully navigate social media to handling rejection, conflict, and peer pressure. Along the way, I encourage you to notice certain passages that resonate with you. The topics in this chapter will address scenarios that tend to trigger anxiety. It's important to keep returning to the skills we've already learned and validate your humanness as we navigate new territory!

PUTTING THE "SOCIAL" IN SOCIAL MEDIA

You're lying on the couch after a long day, scrolling through social media. You just posted a picture of yourself wearing a vintage shirt that you purchased from Goodwill. You consider yourself fashion-forward and are excited to share your unique style. Just then, you receive a notification from a girl in your class. The message reads, "Take that shirt back to Goodwill." Your heart pounds, palms sweat, and chest tightens. Urges to scream and simultaneously crawl into bed race through your mind. You start ruminating and descend into a tailspin of what-ifs. This is accompanied by anger and thoughts that the girls at school don't like you. You start judging yourself, your fashion choices, and your friends.

Sitting in the muddiness of anxiety feels intolerable, so you go for a walk and practice 4-7-8 breathing. Then, you look around and notice three things that you can see, hear, touch, and smell. You begin to feel less anxious; your breath and heart rate slow down. You then check the facts: "What facts do I have in support of and against the thought that the girls don't like me?" You recognize the fact that just one girl commented on your shirt. You remind yourself that just because you think it, doesn't mean it's true.

You list the names of all your friends and people who support you. You hold a half smile as you slowly walk back to your house. As you enter, you resist the urge to catastrophize; you remind yourself that the most likely scenario is probably the most accurate. Once inside, you decide to write an empathetic letter to yourself: "I know this is tough for you right now. I also know you can get through this. Get some sleep. Tomorrow is another day." By dinner that evening, you feel a bit better and decide to delete the girl's comment instead of responding. The next morning, you need a little confidence boost before school. You practice a superhero stance: Stand tall and proud, shoulders back, chin up, and hands at your waist. As you enter homeroom with your vintage shirt on, you inhale and slowly exhale. You know deep inside that you will be okay. It's a new day after all.

SOCIAL MEDIA CLEANUP

Go through your social media profile and take a joy inventory. Delete or silence users and accounts that don't make you feel good about yourself. Add at least three new followers or accounts that increase a healthy mindset (wellness accounts, tips for coping with anxiety, accounts that depict relatable people, or even accounts of cute animals). When we are on our phones or watching TV, we are opening the door to influences. Be mindful of what you choose to let in. We can't control everything, but we can control who and what we follow. Shut the door and say "no" to accounts that don't make you feel good. In the following chart, list which accounts bring you joy, and which ones don't bring you joy.

ACCOUNTS THAT DON'T BRING ME JOY	ACCOUNTS THAT DO BRING ME JOY

UNDER PRESSURE

Your soccer coach has been pushing the team hard lately. We're talking five laps whenever *anyone* shows up even a minute late to practice. Coach has been getting on everyone's nerves, and some of your teammates are angry. You know that he means well and is a good coach, but you're angry, too. *Why does he have to be so strict? Why does he have to push us so hard?*

In the locker room after a particularly hard practice, you hear chatter from your teammates about pulling a prank on Coach. The plan is to lock him in his office. You have mixed feelings about this and know in your gut that it doesn't feel right. The prank could lead to some serious consequences. As angry as you are, you don't want to be involved. However, you feel pressure from your teammates to join in. You start feeling anxious; you're in a tough spot. Your heart pounds and you feel light-headed and jittery. It's hard to catch your breath. You don't want to disappoint your teammates or your coach. You're torn.

You decide to pause and take a minute to gather your thoughts. Then, you take a deep breath and turn to some of your teammates. You look them in the eye, and even though you feel anxious, you announce, "I know Coach is super strict and annoying, but I'm not going to be involved in this prank. I don't think it's a good idea." Some of your teammates look shocked. Some of them giggle, and some listen. Most of them end up agreeing with you, but not all, so the prank is called off. Even though it was incredibly difficult for you to stand up for what you believed in, you did. You pushed through the anxiety wave. You practiced opposite action and "if, then, and" statements. You expressed your needs even though you were experiencing physical sensations of anxiety. You acted in alignment with your core values, and it felt good. You were able to set boundaries, practice assertiveness, and said "no" even with your heart pounding. You realize that having different viewpoints doesn't have to mean losing friendships. You can still fit in and set boundaries. You can stand up for what you believe in, even under pressure.

Read Backward to Lower Anxiety

When you're feeling hijacked by anxiety, this coping strategy works by activating the thinking part of the brain, or "rational mind." All you'll need for this exercise is a short phrase. Now, read that phrase backward, letter by letter, slowly and rhythmically. Repeat as needed.

Example Phrase: *I love unicorns*

Read backward, letter by letter:

s...n...r...o...c...i...n...u...*space****...e...v...o...l...****space****...I***

When we experience anxiety, we activate something called our "emotion mind" which is passionate and emotionally driven. When we problem solve, we activate something called our "rational mind," which is mathematical and logical. In the middle is something called "wise mind," which is a balance between the two mind states. We need all states of mind for different reasons. All three are important. However, it's helpful to know which state we are experiencing to find balance when we need it.

HANDLING REJECTION

You used to be so close to your old neighborhood friends, but those friendships feel distant lately. You're in different classes and have different preferences for activities. You're starting to make new friends, but you still miss your old friends. At gym class, you run track with an old neighborhood friend. You want to be close to them again. As you jog next to them, they seem to ignore you. They choose to speak to their new running buddy instead. You try to catch up and add to their conversation, but they just offer you a smile as they run past you.

You're devastated. You slow down and take a break on the grass. Anxiety, sadness, and anger fill your body, especially in your heart and throat. You worry that you'll lose all your friends. You start looping in all-or-nothing thinking patterns. *The worst-case scenario is sure to happen*, you think. As gym class ends, you distract yourself for the rest of the day until you have time to process the rejection. You practice reading phrases backward, letter by letter. In the bathroom, you splash cold water on your face.

On the bus ride home, you name the speaker of your unhelpful thoughts. You call her Debbie. "Debbie, I hear you, but I don't need your opinion right now. Thanks for visiting." You embrace yourself with a hug and feel comforted. Once home, you lay on your bed and close your eyes. You recall your safe place in vivid detail. You feel the warm sunlight on your arms. You breathe in the smell of seawater. You hear waves crashing in the distance. You feel calm and safe. As you half smile, you remember that just because you were rejected doesn't mean that you don't have friends. You check the facts: Friendships change, and you didn't do anything wrong. Before going downstairs, you give yourself five minutes to feel sensations and emotions like waves in your body. You ask yourself what you need to feel better. At dinner, you ask your dad if he's ever experienced rejection. You actively listen to his response and feel heard in return. You're proud of yourself for practicing skills and reaching out for support. Losing a friend still really hurts, but life's a bit more bearable now. You've changed your mindset and made space to heal.

PROCESSING REJECTION

Make an appointment with yourself to process rejection. In the smaller circle, write all the things that are within your control. In the larger circle, write all the things that are outside your control. To process rejection, we need help taking a step back and changing our perspective. This exercise helps reframe expectations by labeling things that are within and outside our control. Focus all your attention and awareness on the things that are within your control.

Examples of things within our control: *What you eat, what you drink, if you do your homework, how you behave, your words, your ideas, your efforts, how you treat others, how you respond to anxiety, how you dress,* and *your body language.*

Examples of things outside our control: *The weather, the news, what others think about you, what others say about you, events that create stress, how people feel about you, your parents/caregivers, your friends, your family, taxes,* and *laws.*

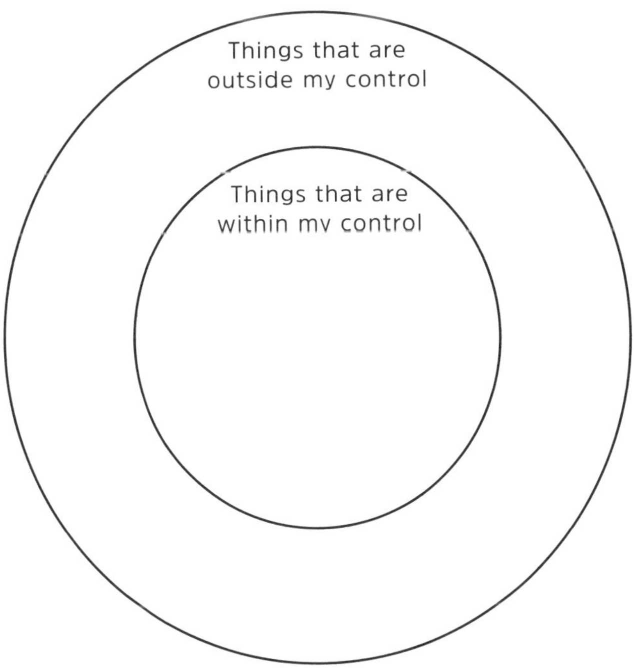

CLASSMATE CONFLICT

You walk into science class take a seat next to a window. The topic excites you: *Ecological Systems of the Galapagos Islands.* You can't wait to participate! The teacher begins by sharing images of animals, plant life, and a short video about the Galapagos. He then turns to the class and asks what they know about Galapagos tortoises.

You raise your hand with enthusiasm and list off facts. The teacher, and most of your classmates, seem impressed. However, Kenny chimes in (as always). He exclaims, "That's actually not true. I've been to the Galapagos before, and the tortoises aren't as big as you say they are." You roll your eyes. You *know* that he probably hasn't been to the Galapagos. However, you're also embarrassed. You start to question what you know. Your face gets hot and red. Your heart beats fast, and your breathing quickens. You're worried that you misspoke. Anxiety and anger start building in your chest and throat. This know-it-all has been interrupting you from day one. However, you stay quiet, cross your arms, and decide not to engage.

You want to put Kenny in his place but decide to address your anxiety first. After practicing progressive muscle relaxation (tensing and then softening muscle groups, one by one) and submerging your face in cold water during your bathroom break, you feel calmer. At the end of class, you approach Kenny and say, "Hey, that was not cool. Can you please not interrupt me?" Kenny responds, "Ugh, it's been a lifelong dream of mine to visit the Galapagos. I'll never have enough money to get there though." You actively listen to him and express empathy, even though you're still annoyed. You respond with open hands and a smile. "I hear you. It's also a lifelong dream of mine to visit the Galapagos, and I'm not sure if I'll make it there either." You both smile at each other. You used this opportunity to practice skills, convey empathy, assert yourself, set a boundary, and actively listen. You showed up authentically and honestly.

Reflection Questions

1. What's one takeaway from this chapter that you found interesting?

____

____

____

2. What's one skill that you are willing to practice from this chapter?

____

____

____

3. What's one thing that you can tell yourself when you face rejection?

____

____

____

Chapter 8

Taking Care (of Yourself and Others)

Skillfully socializing with anxiety requires you to lovingly acknowledge setbacks and show up when you want to hide. This involves a balance between self-soothing and gently approaching anxiety triggers. This new way of socializing places emphasis on changing the way that you respond to anxiety but doesn't change who you are. It invites you to become curious about your perceptions and encourages you to reframe unhelpful dialogue. Above all, it's actively remembering that you are human. You have a permission slip to make mistakes. In this chapter, we'll cover the final pieces to help you build social resilience. This will encompass everything from self-care techniques and building healthy relationships to challenging perfectionism.

DARIUS OPENS THE DOOR

Let's revisit our friend Darius. You may remember him as the artistic teen who really wanted to join the art club. However, anxiety kept him from joining. When we last visited Darius, he didn't have the skills to address his anxiety around socializing. Now, he does. Darius has been practicing 4-7-8 breaths. He's been naming the speaker of his unhelpful thoughts, checking the facts, and practicing opposite action. He's approached a few teens who are in the art club and asked them some questions. He's been challenging the automatic thoughts, becoming more curious about his creative peers in the art club, and offsetting physical sensations of anxiety with progressive muscle relaxation and by reading phrases backward, letter by letter. All this hard work paid off. Darius finally joins the art club. He's entering the art club with his shoulders back, eyes up, and a half smile. He did it!

PRACTICING SELF-LOVE

Anxiety loves self-doubt. It feeds on criticism, unchecked automatic thoughts, and judgments. Therefore, when it comes to managing anxiety in social situations, if we take an active role in caring for our "whole" selves (mind, body, and spirit), the less powerful anxiety becomes. I'll let you in on a little secret. You don't need to love yourself all the time. When you have trouble loving yourself, ask yourself what you might be needing. Then, make a list of all the things that others like about you. You can also note things that you accept about yourself. Start with acceptance first, as self-love grows from acceptance.

REST AND RECHARGE

Putting 100 percent of effort into everything all the time leads to success, right? Not always. Pushing yourself to the limit 24/7 doesn't necessarily lead to success. Don't get me wrong, perseverance, grit, and practice are vital for our growth and learning. However, if we're only driven by how far we can push ourselves, we will burn out. We need to balance our efforts and energy with our wants and needs. In the same way that we recharge our phones, we, too, need to recharge. Thus, I encourage you to adjust. Stop and listen to your body. Notice what it needs. Notice how you feel before and after twenty minutes of rest. Then, check the facts. Will you *really* be more productive with four hours of sleep? Probably not. Along the way, be mindful to not use rest as a form of avoidance; use rest to regulate your emotions and restore energy!

EMBRACE YOUR UNIQUE SPIRIT

We're all born with unique qualities—seedlings that blossom into magnificent trees when nurtured. If we shed light on our seedlings, they will grow. If we water them, they will become stronger. Sometimes, we have trouble trusting ourselves. We question, dislike, or try to hide our uniqueness. However, growth is a process of covering and uncovering our authentic selves. Along the way, remember to resist the urge to compare yourself to other trees, because each tree is plentiful in different ways. Just as trees adapt their growth path toward the light, we, too, can adapt and bend toward the light, even after hiding parts of ourselves in darkness.

CELEBRATE YOUR WINS

Many of us who experience anxiety around socializing tend to focus on what's wrong with us. We can forget what's right with us. We brace ourselves for the worst-case scenario to occur. Small aspects of our social worlds may appear magnified from this vantage point. However, using a broader lens can help you see more clearly. This creates space to acknowledge and celebrate the "whole picture"—including your wins. To make your lens bigger, ask yourself these questions: What's right with me? What's going well in my life right now? Keep an ongoing list of all of your successes, and everything that's going well in your life. You can also add words of gratitude. What are you grateful for? Focus on every tiny win, because those are the elements that create lifelong change. Don't discount what seems insignificant—a smile, a moment of eye contact. Acknowledging your wins is an active way to nurture your seedlings!

SOCIAL PERFECTION ISN'T THE GOAL

Healthy striving is pushing yourself to achieve goals based on your own desires. On the other hand, social perfectionism is an attempt to gain acceptance by putting pressure on yourself to appear perfect. Social perfectionism looks like always agreeing with everyone or trying to do or say the "right" thing. It's avoiding mistakes, criticism, or judgments at all costs. It's concealing parts of yourself and only showing what you think others want to see. There are tools to help us socialize, but we don't want to hide parts of ourselves or focus all our attention on what others want. This, too, needs to be balanced. Trying to be perfect in social situations to alleviate fears of rejection leads to more rejection. People often notice if you're showing up authentically or not. The pressure that you're putting on yourself can be exhausting. Just remember that your friends want to see all of you—the unique, quirky, interesting, and unpolished you. You can practice showing up authentically by noticing the expectations that you're putting on yourself. Practice offering opinions and leave room for mistakes. Challenge your "shoulds" and all-or-nothing thinking. Recognize your wants and needs. Finally, normalize mistakes and set realistic social goals!

ACCENTUATE THE POSITIVE

We will have times when we may not love or even like ourselves. When that happens, try this out. This exercise helps you increase gratitude for parts of your body (and everyday life) that are going/working well. Oftentimes, we take the positives for granted. Beyond this exercise, I highly recommend keeping an ongoing gratitude list, as it's proven to increase a positive mindset:

Step 1: Name three body parts that you're grateful for and label what they do for you:

Example: I am thankful for my feet, which allow me to walk. I am thankful for my eyes, which allow me to see beautiful colors. I am thankful for my ears, which allow me to hear interesting music.

1. ______________________________

2. ______________________________

3. ______________________________

Step 2: Label three qualities that you possess that you are thankful for:

Example: My cooking, my friendliness, my artistic skills

1. ______________________________

2. ______________________________

3. ______________________________

Setting Realistic Expectations

Suffering occurs when expectations don't meet reality. Therefore, if we expect to perform at 100 percent when we're at 60 percent, we set ourselves up for disappointment. Suffering increases when we fail to meet unrealistic expectations. This feeds our anxiety and inner critic. Therefore, start by adjusting your expectations. Label your personal capacity percentage each morning. This percentage will depend on several factors, such as sleep, emotions, events, health, etc. On your best days, you might rate yourself at 100 percent capacity. On your worst days, you might rate yourself at 25 percent capacity. Adjust your expectations to match your personal capacity. For example, if you rate yourself at 75 percent, adjust your expectations so that you're giving 75 percent of effort to tasks. Shift unrealistic tasks to the next day, or tackle what you can. Your best is enough. Remember, we're not condoning avoidance—we're adjusting expectations and the timing of those expectations.

BUILDING BETTER RELATIONSHIPS

Building better relationships starts with respect, compassion, and curiosity toward yourself and others. These elements are the building blocks for feeling safe and connected. Noticing and respecting the time, space, thoughts, and emotions of others is vital to forming stable friendships. It's the framework for trust and closeness, for love and belonging. Based on the practices in this book, you're probably taking small steps toward building trust, compassion, and curiosity within yourself. All of this is great and makes it easier to build better relationships with others. After all, we cannot offer what we don't possess; we cannot pour from an empty cup. Remember that our internal work is helping our external work.

BE CURIOUS

Criticism and judgment are costly. If we had an emotional credit card, it would max out if we only purchased criticism and judgment. On the other hand, curiosity replenishes that credit card. Curiosity helps us learn about others, and learning about others helps us form friendships. When we jump to conclusions and make assumptions, we close doors to information. Curiosity opens doors to information and flexibility. Adopting a curious attitude can even help you reduce anxiety. To start, practice curiosity about everyday items. Look carefully at a pencil or hairbrush. Notice the textures, shapes, and colors. Ponder where it was made and what steps were taken to create the object. Next, start to become curious about your own experiences, and then others around you. Ask yourself questions about other people. This may sound like, "What is their life like and where were they born? Do they ever get nervous about socializing, too?"

SHOW RESPECT

Since respect is the backbone of any relationship, showing respect is one of the first ways that we express care. When I lived in Japan, I had to adapt my body language and mannerisms to show respect in the context of Japanese culture. This included bowing, listening more, and changing the way that I rode public transportation. Expressing respect means allowing personal space when someone needs it. It's not talking over someone, but actively listening. It's agreeing to disagree when you can't see eye to eye. Conveying respect means acknowledging different points of view, choices, and ways of being. It's letting others know that you hear them. Respect means adjusting your body language, tone, or even the way you dress to honor others' values, religion, or culture—even if you don't fully understand it. You don't have to agree with someone to show respect. Respect is the ability to adapt to others' rights and boundaries.

REACH OUT

Reaching out is recognizing struggle in another person and extending a hand. You never really know what someone else is going through. I try to remember this every time I become annoyed with someone. I'm not here to make excuses for unhelpful behaviors, but it's important to recognize that people express struggle in different ways. Some people become anxious, sad, or angry. Some people become bullies, class clowns, or critics. How we treat our peers when they're struggling reflects how we treat ourselves when we struggle. Therefore, reaching out benefits us, too, as it gives us a sense of purpose, belonging, and pride. Our efforts to reach out can be dismissed, but that doesn't mean it wasn't worth it. Every bit of tenderness and kindness we extend to another human being is meaningful and worth it. We may never *really* know the positive impact we have on another person.

KEEP SHINING

Socializing with greater ease consists of daily microscopic actions that bring you just a little bit closer to meaningful connections. It's a half smile. It's noticing a judgment. It's labeling your inner critic. It's being curious about yourself and others. It's focusing on your efforts, not just the outcomes. It's pushing yourself and letting yourself rest. It's surfing the action urges to avoid anxiety and celebrating every win. It's labeling what's right with you. It's asking for help, reaching out for support, checking the facts, and adjusting goals. It's returning to your inner wisdom and breath, over and over. It's challenging unhelpful thoughts. It's showing up imperfectly and letting yourself be seen.

PRACTICING YOUR SOCIAL SKILLS

This exercise will help you reinforce the social skills you've learned throughout this book. Plan to practice two skills per day for two weeks in a row. In the following chart, note the letter(s) that correspond to the skill practiced each day. In the example that follows, on Monday I practiced opposite action **(OA)** and check the facts **(CF)**. On Tuesday I practiced active listening **(AL)** and so on and so forth.

- ***A**pproaching **O**thers* = Walk up and say hello. Ask how someone is doing. Do something nice for someone.
- ***A**ssertive **C**ommunication* = Express your wants and needs while also listening and respecting others' wants and needs, too.
- ***A**ctive **L**istening* = Make eye contact, nod along, listen nonjudgmentally, and resist the urge to interrupt. Pay attention and reflect back what the other person is saying.
- ***R**espect **B**oundaries* = Pay attention to others' body language. Adjust your stance and closeness according to what others need.
- ***C**onfident **B**ody **L**anguage* = Open hands, shoulders back, chin up, soft eye gaze.
- ***H**alf **S**mile* = Upturn the sides of your mouth, like a Mona Lisa smile. Hold for two minutes.
- ***C**heck the **F**acts* = Take note of the evidence for and against a thought or emotional reaction.
- ***O**pposite **A**ction* = If the emotional intensity that you experience doesn't fit the facts, or if it's unhelpful to act on those emotions, act opposite to the urge. Ex: *If you feel intense anger at someone who ignores you, try gently to approach them instead of attacking.*

DAYS OF THE WEEK	MON	TUES	WED	THURS	FRI	SAT	SUN
Examples	OA, CF	AL	RB	AO, AL	HS, OA	HS, CBL	AO, OA
Week #1							
Week #2							

Reflection Questions

1. What does it feel like to get curious about other people?

____

____

2. What does it feel like to read about perfectionism? What came up for you?

____

____

3. What's one way that you can build a better relationship with yourself and others?

____

____

Resources

BOOKS

Conquer Anxiety Workbook for Teens: Find Peace from Worry, Panic, Fear, and Phobias by Tabitha Chansard, PhD

Essential Self-Compassion Workbook for Teens: Overcome Your Inner Critic and Fully Embrace Yourself by Katie Krimer, MA, LCSW

Essential Stress Reduction Workbook for Teens: CBT and Mindfulness Tools to Soothe Stress and Cultivate Calm by Carla Cirilliu Andrews, PsyD

Feeling Better: CBT Workbook for Teens: Essential Skills and Activities to Help You Manage Moods, Boost Self-Esteem, and Conquer Anxiety by Rachel Hutt, PhD

Self-Esteem Tools for Teens: A Modern Guide to Conquer Your Inner Critic and Realize Your True Self-Worth by Megan MacChutcheon, LPC

WEBSITES AND APPS

There are a lot of mental health and wellness resources online, so make sure the sites you visit are written by experts.

Calm
This app offers meditation, music, and movement videos to improve mindfulness practices.
calm.com

Center for Humane Technology
This website offers a youth toolkit with insights about how social media works.
humanetech.com/youth

TEDTalk by Katarina Blom: "You Don't Find Happiness, You Create It"
This talk offers insights on happiness and positive psychology.
youtube.com/watch?v=9DtcSCFwDdw

References

Beck, Judith S. *Cognitive Behavior Therapy: Basics and Beyond, 3rd edition.* New York: Guilford Press, 2020.

Brady, Mark. *Noble Listening.* Whitby Island, WA: CreateSpace Independent Publishing Platform, 2015.

Brewer, Judson MD PhD. *Unwinding Anxiety*. New York: Penguin Random House, 2013.

Firth, Chris. "Role of Facial Expressions in Social Interactions." *Philosophical Transactions of the Royal Society: Biological Sciences* 364, no. 1535 (December 2009). doi.org/10.1098/rstb.2009.0142.

Hanh, Thich Nhat. *No Mud, No Lotus: The Art of Transforming Suffering*. Berkeley, CA: Parallax Press, 2014.

Houston, Elaine B.Sc. "Introvert vs Extrovert: A Look at the Spectrum and Psychology." *Positive Psychology*. April 2, 2019. positivepsychology.com/introversion-extroversion-spectrum.

Hutcherson, Will, and Chinwé Williams, PhD, LPC. *Seen: Healing Despair and Anxiety in Kids and Teens through the Power of Connection.* Cumming, GA: Parent Cue, 2021.

Keltner, Dacher. "The Compassionate Instinct." *Greater Good Magazine*. March 1, 2004. greatergood.berkeley.edu/article/item/the_compassionate_instinct.

König, Nicola, Sarah Steber, Josef Seebacher, Quinten Von Prittwitz, Harald R. Bliem, and Sonja Rossi. "How Therapeutic Tapping Can Alter Neural Correlates of Emotional Prosody Processing in Anxiety" *Brain Sciences* 9, no. 8 (August 2019): 206. doi.org/10.3390/brainsci9080206.

Levine, Peter A., with Ann Frederick. *Waking the Tiger: Healing Trauma.* Berkeley, CA: North Atlantic Books, 1997.

Linehan, Marsha M. *DBT Skills Training Handouts and Worksheets.* New York: Guilford Press, 2014.

Neff, Kristin D., and Christopher K. Germer. "A Pilot Study and Randomized Controlled Trial of the Mindful Self-Compassion Program." *Journal of Clinical Psychology* vol. 69, no. 1 (October 2012):1–17. onlinelibrary.wiley.com/doi/10.1002/jclp.21923.

Ortega, Alejandra "Grammar: Active and Passive Voice." Purdue OWL. February 1, 2019. Video, 4:22. youtube/GEP-8IFTKKg.

Seligman, Martin E. P. *The Optimistic Child*. New York: Houghton Mifflin Company, 1995.

Soto-Icaza, Patricia, Francisco Aboitiz, and Pablo Billeke. "Development of Social Skills in Children: Neural and Behavioral Evidence for the Elaboration of Cognitive Models." *Frontiers in Neuroscience* 9 (September 2015): 333. doi.org/10.3389/fnins.2015.00333.

van der Kolk, Bessel. *The Body Keeps the Score: Brain, Mind, and Body in the Healing of Trauma*. New York: Penguin Books, 2015.

Weil, Andrew. "Breathing Exercises: 4-7-8 Breath." DrWeil.com.drweil .com/videos-features/videos/breathing-exercises-4-7-8-breath.

Yang, Tony T. MD, PhD, Alan N. Simmons PhD, Scott C. Matthews MD, Susan F. Tapert PhD, et al. "Increased Amygdala Activation Is Related to Heart Rate During Emotion Processing in Adolescent Subjects." *Neuroscience Letters* 428, no. 2–3 (November 2007): 109-114. doi.org/10.1016/j.neulet.2007.09.039.

Index

ACKNOWLEDGMENTS

I'd like to thank my husband, Zack, for his unwavering patience and unapologetic love and for the precious gift of time that allowed me to write this book. My mother and father, for their unbridled support of my career path, and my three spirited children, Chloe, Ella, and Ollie, for inspiring me to be a better human every day. Finally, I'd like to thank my sisters, Lizzy and Cat, for being my cheerleaders. To my clients, for helping me grow and learn.

ABOUT THE AUTHOR

Emily Davenport is a licensed creative arts therapist, board-certified art therapist, and the founder of Davenport Creative Arts Therapy, PLLC, in New York City and Westchester County. Over the past fourteen years, Emily has served as a group therapist, individual therapist, clinical supervisor, and consultant. She's intensively trained in dialectical behavior therapy (DBT) and helped spearhead DBT-informed curriculum for tweens and teens within New York State's Office of Mental Health system. She specializes in treating anxiety disorders, treatment-resistant depression, and C-PTSD. Emily has been featured in numerous podcasts and media outlets. She's a member of the American Art Therapy Association, New York Art Therapy Association, and New York University's Graduate Art Therapy Advisory Committee. For more information, visit DavenportCreativeArtsTherapy.com.